THE BEST OF
WARNER BROS.

1

2

3

4

5

THE BEST OF
WARNER BROS.

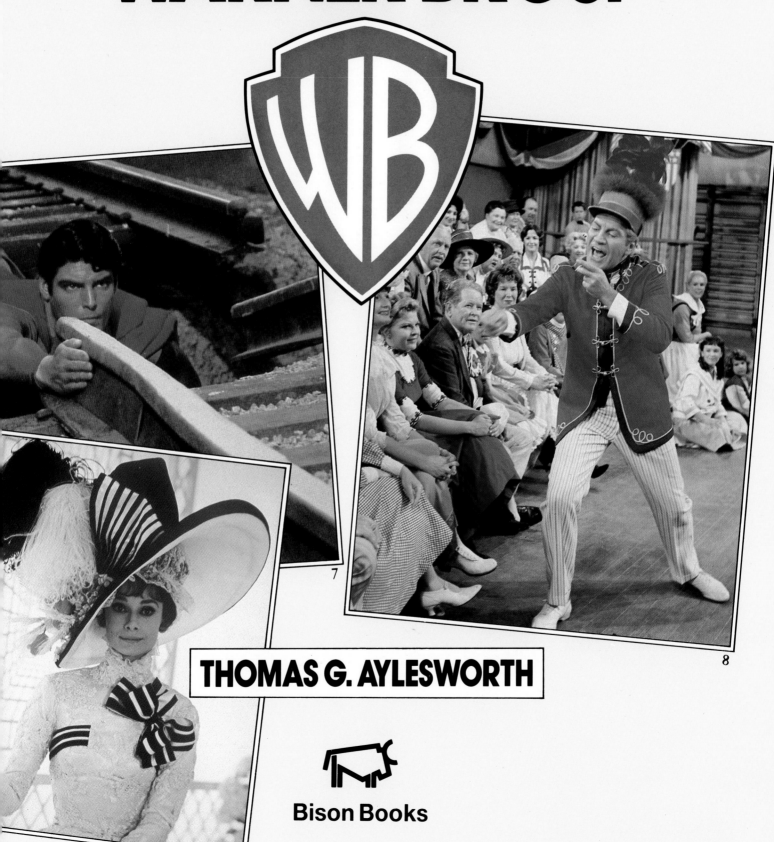

THOMAS G. AYLESWORTH

Bison Books

First Published in 1986 by
Bison Books Ltd
176 Old Brompton Road
London SW5
England

ISBN 0 86124 268 8

Printed in Hong Kong

Previous spread:
1. *A chorus number from* Dames *(1934)*.
2. *A theater poster* – The Jazz Singer *(1927)*.
3. The Maltese Falcon *(1941) with Bogart*.
4. The Treasure of the Sierra Madre *(1948)*.
5. *Edward G Robinson* – Little Caesar *(1930)*.
6. *Audrey Hepburn* – My Fair Lady *(1964)*.
7. *Christopher Reeve* – Superman *(1978)*.
8. *Robert Preston* – The Music Man *(1962)*.

CONTENTS

PREFACE

WARNER BROS. HAS LONG been known as 'the working man's studio,' partly because it seemed to specialize in pictures that would appeal to the common folk and partly because it ground out so many films – many of them excellent, many of them pretty bad – in the first three-quarters of a century that the studio has been in existence. There have been thousands of them, far too many to be mentioned in a book of this length. So some choices had to be made about which movies to include and which to leave out.

A book filled with Warner triumphs, and there have been many, would be boring. So, in addition to the triumphs, some of the lesser-known or forgotten films have been included, providing they had something going for them – a new photographic process, a new actor or actress who was to become a legend, a bit of behind-the-scenes gossip.

But what to leave out? Obviously, absolutely rotten films with no redeeming value head the list. And there are the purely exploitation movies such as the *Kung Fu* releases and the *Cleopatra Jones* series that fall into this category. Actually, because of lack of space, series films have been left out altogether. Warners made plenty of those, but they were quickies, well done ones, but nevertheless quickies, most of them made to fill the bottom half of a double bill. Thus some very entertaining claptrap had to be jettisoned, such as the immensely popular *Nancy Drew* films with Bonita Granville, the *Torchy Blane* movies with Glenda Farrell, the *Perry Mason* and *Philo Vance* mysteries with Warren William and the *Penrod* pictures with Billy and Bobby Mauch, those appealing Hollywood twins.

And because, by and large, when a sequel of a blockbuster is made, it fails to live up to the quality of the original, these films have been also eliminated. Out went the subsequent *Dirty Harry* movies with Clint Eastwood (alas), as well as such inferior products as *Brother Rat and A Baby* (1940), *The Angels Wash Their Faces* (1939) and *Exorcist II: The Heretic* (1977).

Warner Bros. has also made many films in cooperation with foreign film makers and imported for release in the United States many more, especially from Hammer in England and Toho in Japan. But there would not be room to list all of these unless they were particularly meritorious.

Finally, the wonderful cartoon shorts from Warners deserve a separate book by themselves, and could not be accommodated here. So goodbye, Bugs Bunny, Elmer Fudd, Sylvester, Tweetie Pie, Pepe la Pew, Yosemite Sam and The Roadrunner.

Those are the guidelines. Now on with the show.

Thomas G. Aylesworth
Stamford, Connecticut

Jack Warner and one of his greatest stars – Rosalind Russell.

IN THE
BEGINNING

IT ALL BEGAN IN 1879 IN the small Polish village of Krasnashiltz, near the German border, when Pearl Warner, the wife of Benjamin Warner, a poor cobbler, gave birth to her first child. They named him Harry, and by the time that his sister, Anna, was born in 1881, the Warners realized that they could no longer endure the ghastly conditions in the Jewish ghetto, and Benjamin left his family to travel on a cattle boat to the United States. He settled in Baltimore and hoped to send for his family later.

Benjamin, being a cobbler, naturally opened a small shoe store in that city, where he lived in a slum – always saving his money in order to be reunited with Pearl and the two children. He didn't do badly, and in some weeks he was able to earn two or three dollars. But he started making more money when, exhibiting an entrepreneurial skill that would pop up in the next generation, he invented the idea of repairing shoes while the customers waited. After a year he was able to send for Pearl, Harry and Anna. The family moved to South Baltimore, and then the new babies began arriving like popcorn – Albert was born in 1884, and then came Henry, Samuel, Rose and Fannie. Henry and Fannie, however, died when they were toddlers. The remaining children were soon earning money by doing odd jobs, selling newspapers and shining shoes. Benjamin, thinking that the business was such a success that he could be spared from it, decided to travel through the country selling pots and pans while Pearl and the children looked after the shop.

But something happened to Benjamin that was not unlike the problems encountered by the citizens' band radio manufacturers in the 1970s and the home computer makers in the 1980s. It turned out that everyone who needed pots and pans already had pots and pans, so Benjamin went north to the less

settled areas of Canada to trade his pots and pans for animal furs and pelts, which he then sold in the towns. Enthusiastic over his prospects, he sold his Baltimore shop and took his family north in a wagon. Meanwhile, he was double-crossed by a partner, and the family found itself penniless in Canada. Still, two more sons were born to Pearl and Benjamin – Jack in London, Ontario in 1892 and David, in Hamilton, Ontario in 1893.

The family then went back to Baltimore where Benjamin started to resurrect his cobbling business. By 1896, 15-year-old Harry and 12-year-old Albert were such good shoe repairmen that the family moved to Youngstown, Ohio – where they felt there were wider opportunities – to begin the business again. Their shop became a success because of their skills, but then it became a failure, also because of their skills. They were making their shoes so well that the shoes lasted for a long time before they needed repair, and once again the family felt the cold hands of poverty.

Benjamin then decided to add a small grocery to his shoe shop, but that was not a success since it was no different than many other mom and pop stores in the neighborhood. So he rented a bigger store in Youngstown's Polish section, selling both groceries and meats. By this time, a daughter, Sadye, and a son, Milton, had been born. Jack was put in charge of the deliveries for the store, but he had become something of a performer and actor, and spent some of his time entertaining anyone who would stop to watch. He hung out at carnivals, fairs and benefit nights at the Young Men's Christian Association, where he was a boy soprano very much in demand. Finally he broke into show business legitimately when he landed a job singing the song slides at a downtown Youngstown theater. Later he was booked for a tour of

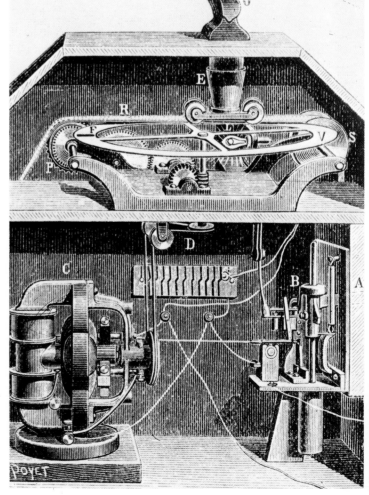

theaters in Ohio and Pennsylvania. This was in 1907 and he was only 15 years old.

Albert had moved to Chicago in 1900, where he became a soap salesman, and Harry was the financial advisor at the store in Youngstown. Harry didn't really care much for the grocery business, but he certainly turned out to have a flair for negotiation.

Sam, too, went into show business. He became a barker in a carnival and fronted for a snake charmer. But when one of the pythons tried to strangle the charmer, the show was closed and Sam became an ice-cream cone salesman. That didn't pay much, so he became a fireman on the Erie Railroad. Sam didn't stay with the railroad for long, but rather learned to operate an Edison Kinetoscope and became a projectionist in the White City Amusement Park in Chicago, showing a travelogue on Yosemite National Park. Enthusiastic about the machine, Sam returned to Youngstown and was able to convince his family that movies were the thing of the future.

It was Benjamin who was really convinced. He pawned his watch, his watchchain and his horse to buy a Model B Projector. The family rented an empty store in Niles, Ohio, and showed a print of *The Great Train Robbery*, which was a sellout. Rose played the piano, Albert and Harry ran the box office and Jack sang illustrated songs. Their first week's take was a monumental $300.

The Great Train Robbery (1903) was a phenomenon of the early part of this century. Produced by the Edison Company, it was a one-reeler with a running time of about 12 minutes. It cast little more than flickering shadows on the screen and boasted a plot that no one, not even the most backward and backwater of audiences, could ever call mentally taxing. Yet this relic stands as one of the most influential films ever made. A smash hit at the Nickelodeon box offices, it breathed life into a dying infant industry and started the American movie business on its way to becoming an industry that, within three decades, would be taking in 110 million admissions a week. Of even greater consequence, *Robbery* gave birth to one of the most enduring of the film genre – the Western, the horse opera, the oater, the cowboy picture.

The Great Train Robbery attracted audiences on two counts. People were, to begin with, fascinated to see what they thought to be the rugged western outdoors, although they were badly mistaken here because *Robbery*'s exteriors were shot just a few miles outside New York City in the 'wilds' surrounding Paterson, New Jersey. But what counted more was the fact that, against this pleasing outdoor backdrop, *Robbery* told a story that – to borrow one of the most venerable of film advertising clichés – was 'action-packed' from start to finish. The combination of action and the outdoors was chemistry that would work for years to come.

And there was unremitting action, no doubt about it. *The Great Train Robbery* opens with four bandits entering a rural railroad depot and sandbagging the telegraph operator. After binding him and gagging him, they move outside, take over a train that is stopping for water, rob the mail car and the passengers, shoot one of the trainmen and put a bullet in a

passenger who attempts to escape. Forcing the engineer to uncouple the locomotive from the rest of the cars, they steam away with the loot, soon jumping clear and dashing to their horses in a nearby wood. The telegraph operator and his daughter, who has happened on the scene of the crime, make their way to a barn dance where they enlist a posse. The posse gallops off, tracks down the bandits and kills them as they celebrate over their 'take.' And, in about 12 minutes, that's about all that the traffic will bear.

The picture ends in a surprising fashion. After the story has been told, one of the bandits (actor George Barnes) is seen in a closeup with his hat pushed back on his head. He stares at the camera, raises his six-gun and fires a shot at the audience. It was a moment that had nothing whatsoever to do with the rest of the film. According to an Edison catalogue of its then-current productions, theater managers were free to use the sequence at the beginning or the end of the film. Apparently it was in imitation of the distinctive photographs that had long been the opening and closing features of lantern slide shows.

Flicker though its images do, *The Great Train Robbery* is a well made, entertaining movie. The credit for its quality must go to its director, Edwin S Porter, acknowledged as possibly the most skilled and inventive of the early American movie makers. His skill is seen in the momentum and excitement he gives the picture by refusing to allow his camera, at least after the opening sequences, to photograph the players in the static fashion of the day, as if they are being viewed on a stage. Rather, he follows them about in true cinematic style, a chief example here being the lengthy pan shot that tracks the bandits through the woods after they have abandoned the locomotive.

His inventiveness is seen in his continuous use of intercutting, the device that enables him to discover simultaneous actions in different locales and even, at one point, to jump backwards a few moments in time. Then he introduces the ellipsis, the now familiar leap forward in time by the omission of nonessential material. Rather than following the telegrapher and his daughter to the barn dance where the posse is to be conscripted, Porter cuts directly to the dance and then has the two principals enter. It has been said that Porter stumbled on the ellipsis by accident, resorting to it because he was running out of film stock. Perhaps. Necessity, as the old saying goes, has always been the mother of invention. If so in this case, it gave us what has now become one of the most basic film techniques.

In addition to its excellent pacing, *Robbery* contains some individual moments of fine drama – the bandits, threateningly quiet, as they force the engineer to uncouple the locomotive, and then their almost acrobatic falls when they are shot in the closing scenes. There is a particularly memorable moment when, through intercutting, Porter builds suspense with glimpses of the bandits' tethered horses nervously awaiting the return of their masters. And who can forget that rowdy barn dance sequence when a collection of western toughs, soon to become the posse, make a tenderfoot 'dance' as they fire their six-guns at his feet? It was fare that, transferred to saloons, was to become a staple on many a future western movie.

In fact, Porter was able to get into *The Great Train Robbery*'s 12 minutes all but a few of what were to be the basic ingredients of the cowboy movie. The splendid histrionics of the wagon train closing into a circle when attacked and the nick-of-time arrival of the cavalry were to come later

Two more scenes from The Great Train Robbery *(1903).*
Opposite: *After overpowering the train crew, the bandits force the engineer to uncouple the locomotive from the train. They will soon use the engine for their getaway vehicle, taking the loot with them.*

Right: *The final closeup of bandit George Barnes as he faces the audience just before he fires his famous six-gun shot at the paying customers.*

with the westward-trek epics of the 1920s. But the truly basic wares – the good guys, the bad guys, the wrong-doing, the chase and the final showdown – are all present in *The Great Train Robbery*.

While there is no argument that, contrary to legend, *The Great Train Robbery* was not the first picture to tell a story but only the first Western to do so, the film does rightly deserve the other honor that has been bestowed on it – that of being 'America's first real movie.' It was, indeed, a real movie, excitingly photographed, fast paced, and quick and mobile in its time and locale shifts. The pace that Porter gave it and the inventiveness that he brought to it made it actual cinema fare and not a stage play recorded on film.

No wonder the Warners made so much money with it.

After their success in Niles, Sam and Albert toured Ohio and Pennsylvania with the show. Their big problem was that by the time the tour had ended, the fragile print of *The Great Train Robbery* had broken and was mended so many times that the plot line was almost unintelligible. But the tour had been such a success that Harry, Sam and Albert went to Newcastle, Pennsylvania, the site of their biggest triumph on the tour, rented chairs from an undertaker and opened their own Cascade Theater, showing films rented in Pittsburgh. Here they used a wonderful gimmick. As the movie was being rewound, Jack would take the stage and recite poetry. Naturally the poetry served to help clear the theater of patrons – and they left in droves – so that the second show could begin with a new audience.

By 1908 the Warner Brothers were so successful that they owned some 200 films and were also making money renting them to other theaters all over western Pennsylvania. Their office operated out of Pittsburgh and the Warners were able to set up other exchanges in Norfolk, Virginia, and Atlanta, Georgia.

By 1909 there were thousands of theaters in the United States and the Warners were doing quite well. But then the roof caved in.

The great inventor, Thomas Alva Edison, although a certified genius, also turned out to be a shrewd business man. Of course he had been a pioneer in the movie business, but he discovered that he was not getting a share in the money being made by the exhibitors, so he talked to the major movie studios of the time – Vitagraph, Selig, Essanay, Biograph, Lubin and Kalem in the United States, and Pathé and Méliès in France – and they formed the Motion Picture Patents Company. 'The Trust,' as the organization became known, prevented independent producers from making films without a license. Nor could exchanges, such as the Warners', distribute their films. Those theaters who used the Trust's pictures would be charged two dollars per week for each projector they used. Also, the General Film Company was formed to buy out exhibitors. All of this forced the Warners to sell their exchanges.

But then Sam came to the rescue. He bought the rights for a five reel film version of *Dante's Inferno* in New York and took it on the road with a narrator who read from the original poem. At the end of the tour, the Warners had netted the unbelievable sum of $1500. Unfortunately Sam and Jack lost it all in a New York crap game.

Jack, Sam, Albert and Harry, however, had just enough money to follow Harry's suggestion that they make a couple of two reelers in a hurry. They rented an abandoned foundry in St Louis which they turned into a studio and Jack wrote a scenario about Indians and settlers, calling it *Peril of the*

Plains (1910). Starring Dot Farley, a Chicago non-actress who could ride a horse, it was completed in three days. Sam, the director of *Peril on the Plain*, also directed their second quickie, *Raiders on the Mexican Border* (1910). Neither of these films was what might be called, even with the most charitable motives, a success.

But Carl Laemmle, who would later become the head of Universal Studios in their palmiest days, was fighting The Trust by forming the Independent Motion Picture Company to distribute films by himself and from other non-Trust exchanges. The Warners gave him their support in 1912 and Sam was sent to Los Angeles and Jack to San Francisco to form new distribution exchanges. The Warners prospered with the release of such films as *War Brides* (1916).

The idea of rebellious women served not as a partial theme, as had been done so many times before, but as the very basis of *War Brides*. Produced by Lewis Selznick (the father of David O Selznick of *Gone With the Wind* fame) and starring Alla Nazimova, the film was set in an imaginary kingdom and told the story of a young woman named Joan whose husband is killed when the kingdom goes to war. Despondent, Joan thinks first of committing suicide and then, for the sake of her unborn child, decides to go on living, only to hear that the king has decreed that young married women must mate with soldiers leaving for the front. Angered that she and her kind are being forced to bear future cannon fodder, Joan calls for the women around her to disobey the

edict. She is arrested and condemned to death, with her sentence then changed to life imprisonment when her pregnancy is discovered. In the final sequences, Joan escapes from her cell and marshals the women to protest the war when the king makes a public appearance.

With fine performances by Alla Nazimova, Richard Barthelmess and a solid supporting cast, *War Brides* was both a financial and critical success and was much praised for its idealism. The only sour critical note was centered on its plot development, a problem caused by the fact that it was based on a 15-minute stage play and so, to come up with a screen running time of 80 minutes, had been considerably padded. Because of its anti-war sentiments, it was immediately withdrawn from circulation when the United States entered its period of neutrality in the spring of 1917.

Despite its withdrawal, the film made money for the Warner Brothers, even though they had paid the astronomical fee of $50,000 for the right to distribute it in California, Nevada and Arizona alone.

Flushed with success, they paid $100,000 for the distribution rights for a Selig film, *The Crisis* (1917). This was a flop. It was a Civil War film, and was released on 5 April 1917. The next day the United States declared war on Germany and the American public found that it didn't want to watch a war movie.

At this time, Harry was still in New York and had not given up. He bought the rights to a story called 'Passions Inherited' by Ella Wheeler Wilcox for $15,000 and commissioned director Gilbert P Hamilton to shoot the film in southern California. It was expected to be filmed in five weeks, but Hamilton ran off with one of the extras and Jack had to edit what had been shot. He was a novice at editing, but his reuse of several scenes at the beginning of the film and at its end, he claimed, were never detected. The film barely broke even, however, just like the company's two previous efforts.

The Warners' first try at a really major feature film came in 1918 with *My Four Years in Germany*. Jack had bought a copy of the memoirs of James W Gerard, who was the United States Ambassador to Germany from 1913 to 1917, which recounted how he tried to get Kaiser Wilhelm II to abandon submarine warfare. He got the rights for $50,000 and the film was made and then released by First National. The movie was a winner, grossing $1,500,000, giving the Warner Brothers a $13,000 profit after they had paid off the loans and other expenses.

They advertised the film as 'Fact, not fiction,' and it was filmed as a semi-documentary. The company also maintained that it was made with a compilation of newsreel films taken in German prison camps, although the movie was shot entirely in the United States. At any rate, part of its success was due to a lot of violence, which was as popular then as it is now, and its anti-German sentiments were good propaganda material for a nation at war. In the film, the Germans could be blamed for anything – like the Indians in Westerns, they had no way to complain.

Some of the subtitles were classics. Hindenburg says of the population of Belgium: 'Healthy ones to the farms; use your discretion with young and old.' A Belgian girl says to Gerard:

'We are slaves.' The exteriors in the film were shot in upstate New York and the interiors at the Biograph Studios in the Bronx. Gerard actually played himself in the movie.

The Kaiser's Finish was another Warner opus of 1918. In this one, the illegitimate American-reared son of the Kaiser enters Germany to kill his father and the Crown Prince. In the film were newsreel shots of the prince, as one critic said, 'just standing around looking foolish.' The film starred Earl Shenck and Claire Whitney, and not much has been heard of it since.

Their success led the Warner Brothers to build a studio of their own in 1919, rather than renting space from other companies, such as the borrowed facility where they shot two serials starring Helen Holmes – *The Lost City* and *The Tiger's Claw*. The new studio was located at Sunset and Bronson. It covered ten acres and was called Warner Brothers West Coast Studio. The price was $25,000 plus $1500 per month. The Brothers divided up the work: Harry ran the business from New York, Albert was the treasurer (answerable to Harry) and Jack and Sam ran the movie-making side. The only problem was that the studio lacked something essential – real creative talent.

One of their last productions before the new studio was opened was *Open Your Eyes* (1919), which had been made at the Biograph Studios in the Bronx in 1917. Jack even appeared in the movie, which was a pretty racy picture, being an educational film dealing with venereal disease. Jack was an American soldier who was sold a worthless bottle of medicine for ten dollars and finds himself overcome with disease. Needless to say, this was the end of Jack's acting career, but one actor who was in the film got a leg up on his acting career – Ben Lyon. Warners made the picture for the United States Army Signal Corps, but kept the commercial rights. They never made a profit on the film.

But with their new studio and their new found-clout in the business, the 1920s were to be a decade of challenge.

Opposite: *Alla Nazimova protects a young girl from the lustful advances of an army officer in* War Brides *(1916).*

Below: *A view of the entrance to the old Warner Bros. studio in 1925, two years after it had been expanded.*

THE
TWENTIES

BY THE DAWN OF THE 1920S Hollywood was well embarked on the star system. Among the great actors and actresses in their glory at this time were Charlie Chaplin, Mary Pickford, Douglas Fairbanks Sr, Harold Lloyd, Lon Chaney Sr, Gloria Swanson, Pola Negri, Lillian and Dorothy Gish, Alla Nazimova, Colleen Moore, Buster Keaton, John Barrymore and Rudolph Valentino. Some of these people actually made more than $5000 per week.

The early part of the decade was also the time of the immigration to Hollywood of some of the top European directors and producers, such as Ernst Lubitsch, F W Murnau, Paul Leni, Michael Curtiz and Mauritz Stiller. Lubitsch was to make five pictures for Warners in the 1920s – *The Marriage Circle* (1924), *Three Women* (1924), *Kiss Me Again* (1925), *Lady Windermere's Fan* (1925), *So This Is Paris* (1926) – and Curtiz made two – *The Third Degree* (1926) and *Noah's Ark* (1928).

The 1920s started out on a small scale for Warner Brothers. The new studio turned out a mere three feature pictures in 1921 and four in 1922, but things started to change in 1923. After the Warner Brothers West Coast Studio name was changed to the simple Warner Bros. in that year, the brothers spent $250,000 in redoing the plant and adding a huge new stage measuring 420 feet by 140 feet, making it possible to shoot six films at one time.

Warner Bros., who had made 17 features in 1924, upped the number to 31 in 1925 – four of them with Rin-Tin-Tin (*Tracked in the Snow Country, Below the Line, Class of the Wolves* and *Lighthouse by the Sea*). In 1926, the number of feature films went up to 33, and in 1927 a record 43 features were released by Warner Bros. The big one, of course, was *The Jazz Singer*, but the Warner stars kept making money for the studio – Monte Blue was in seven films, Irene Rich and May McAvoy in six, Warner Oland and Myrna Loy in five and Rin-Tin-Tin, Ben Lyon and Dolores Costello in four.

With the success of *The Jazz Singer* (1927, and more about that later), Warners had to expand to make more sound movies. They knew it was the coming thing and were proved right just two years later, when more than 9000 theaters in the United States had installed sound equipment. Warners built a larger sound stage and by the end of 1928 were able to supply some 400 theaters in the United States with sound films. In September of 1928, with $100,000,000 it had borrowed, the studio bought the Stanley Corporation of America, a theater chain with over 250 theaters in 75 cities and seven states. That ensured a wide distribution for Warner Bros. movies. In October, the studio bought First National Pictures, which also owned a theater chain. Jack Warner was now head of production, with Darryl F Zanuck as his right hand man, and the company moved into the First National Studios, after first wiring them for sound production. By buying First National, Warners also acquired the contracts for such stars as Colleen Moore, Douglas Fairbanks Jr, Billie Dove, Loretta Young, the Talmadge Sisters, Richard Barthelmess, Harry Langdon, Basil Rathbone and Constance Bennett. By November of 1928, the brothers had paid off all their outstanding bank loans.

Left: *A scene at the world premiere of a Vitaphone sound picture. Left to right: Harry M Warner, president of Warner Bros.; Will Hays, president of The Motion Picture Producers and Distributors of America (soon to become the official censor of the movies with his 'Hays Office'); Walter C Rich, president of the Vitaphone Corporation and Sam L Warner, vice-president of Warner Bros. and the Vitaphone Corporation.*

Opposite: *Marie Prevost is approached by the lecherous Kenneth Harlan in* The Beautiful and Damned *(1922).*

Previous spread: *Al Jolson as Jakie Rabinowitz and May McAvoy as Mary Dale, the showgirl who loves him, in* The Jazz Singer *(1927).*

Financially, 1929 was a complicated year for Warner Bros. Fox West Coast Theaters still owned one-third interest in First National. But Fox was in debt, so it sold its interest to Warners in November for $10,000,000, and that meant that Warners owned First National completely. In 1929, Warner Bros. released 86 feature films – 45 of them as First National Pictures. The company also bought the music firm of Remick, Harms and Witmark, with its vast collection of musical copyrights, and Harry's son Lewis was put in charge of the operation. Finally, at the first ever Academy Awards dinner, Warner Bros. was presented with a special Oscar for producing *The Jazz Singer*.

Warners made only one film in 1920, and it was not a feature film, but rather a serial in 15 episodes called *A Dangerous Adventure*. Jack and Sam directed it and hired a complete traveling circus for it as well as signing Grace Darmond and Derelys Perdue to play the parts of two sisters in search of hidden treasure in Darkest Africa. The story was predictable, but offscreen Jack was attacked by a monkey, an elephant wrecked the set and the two leading ladies acted like jealous *prima donnas*. The film was a flop at first but in 1922, edited down to seven reels from 30, it became a feature film, and was a hit.

Probably the most popular of Warner Bros. 1921 films was *Why Girls Leave Home*, starring Anna Q Nilsson. The theme

was one that Jack Warner loved and one that would be used by him time after time – the corruption of an innocent by the big city.

Another production of 1921 was *Your Best Friend*, which told of a Jewish mother (Vera Gordon) who is spurned by her son's Gentile wife (shades of the upcoming *The Jazz Singer*). But the wife finds that she and her husband are really being supported by the mother, and she learns to love the old woman. Audiences forgot the possible motive of greed, and believed that the daughter-in-law had turned over a new leaf.

Rags to Riches (1921) was Wesley Barry's first film. He played a rich kid, Marmaduke Clarke, who endures all kinds of perils before he is accepted by the local gang. The film was important for only two reasons – Barry's debut and the urban environment in the movie which the studio handled so well in its future crime movies and social dramas of the 1930s.

Ashamed of Parents (1922) was one of the first social dramas to appear on American screens. It might have been modeled on the lives of the Warner Brothers themselves. Silas Wadsworth, a shoemaker, struggles to send his son to college. The son becomes a football star. And that's about it, except that the point was made that even if one comes from a low and humble beginning, one can still conquer the world.

The Beautiful and Damned (1922), the first screen version of F Scott Fitzgerald's 'lost generation,' depicted the youth of 1922 as irresponsible, crazy and hard-drinking. The important thing about the film was that Marie Prevost and Louise Fazenda, both former Max Sennett bathing beauties, were making their first film for Warners. Otherwise, it had little to recommend it, since Sidney Franklin directed it as a movie that began as fun but started taking itself too seriously and began sermonizing.

School Days (1922) was inspired by the classic Gus Edwards song and was another film about the corrupting influences of the big city. It starred Wesley Barry, who played a boy who came from a small town to the big town and is led down the primrose path. He does, however, find redemption in the last reel, and returns to his origins.

Warner Bros. was later to have the patent on the gangster film, and *Parted Curtain* (1922) was probably their first effort in that genre. Henry B Walthall, an actor best known for his role of 'the Little Colonel' in Griffith's *Birth of A Nation*, played the part of a convict who cannot find a job after serving his time in prison. He steals money from a painter, who feels compassion and tries to rehabilitate him.

Harry Warner bought the rights to three plays in 1923: *The Gold Diggers* by Avery Hopwood, *Deburau* by Sacha Guitry and *Daddies* by David Belasco. All of this was done for a total price of $250,000.

It was *The Gold Diggers* (1923), although it was a silent movie, that planted the seed of making films from Broadway musicals in the heads of the Warner Brothers. David Belasco had produced the Hopwood play on Broadway and his name flickering on the screen brought huge audiences into the theaters. The story line was one of the first ones to utilize the idea of a couple of New York showgirls on the make. Louise Fazenda and Hope Hampton were the girls, one of whom sacrifices everything in order that her sister can marry the man she loves. Also in the cast were Wyndham Standing and Jed Prouty.

The studio then came out with another gangster film, *Heroes of the Street* (1923). Starring Wesley Barry, it told of a young boy who tries to solve the murder of his father, a policeman. Marie Prevost and Jack Mulhall costarred.

Barry made another 1923 picture, co-starring with Harry Myers. It was about a couple of kids who put out a newspaper, *The Briggsville Gazette*. Things go along nicely until Myers is arrested for a robbery he did not commit (sound familiar?). Of course, Barry is able to find the real criminal.

Little Johnny Jones (1923) was another silent musical released by the studio. It was based on George M Cohan's 1904 Broadway musical and told the story of an English earl's decision to enter an American horse in the Epsom Derby. The earl was played by Wyndham Standing and his American jockey, Johnny Jones, was played by Johnny Hines. But the movie desperately needed the sparkle of the sprightly Cohan songs.

Another David Belasco film, *Tiger Rose* (1923), was a solid adaptation of Belasco's play of the same name, and was a handsome movie – filmed in the Canadian Northwest. Lenore Ulric played the title role – a girl who shoots a mountie in order to protect her lover. The problem was that this film was too much like another movie, *The Girl of the Golden West*, which was released earlier that same year by First National.

The highlight of 1923 was the first appearance of one of the most successful actors in the history of movies – Rin-Tin-Tin. This German shepherd first starred in *Where the North Begins*. The wonder dog played himself, of course, a dog who was adopted by wolves but saves the life of a fur trapper. Warners had found its first certifiable box office star. Rinty went on to make 19 movies at a salary of $1000 per week. He was also supplied with a small orchestra to play mood music, a diamond-studded collar and huge steaks at mealtime.

The Marriage Circle (1924) marked the beginning of Ernst Lubitsch's association with Warner Bros. – an association that lasted for five films. The German-born Lubitsch, a successful stage actor and screen director in Europe before coming to Hollywood to direct Mary Pickford in *Rosita* (1923), was undoubtedly one of the most impressive of the early film directors. The fact is, he was impressive in any assignment he took on, whether it was a musical, a drama or a comedy. It was, however, in comedy – and its musical counterpart – that he earned his greatest fame, displaying both a talent for satire and a deft ability for handling sophisticated themes. Indeed, he put his stamp on anything he did – a stamp that was to become known as 'The Lubitsch Touch.'

Lubitsch films, from beginning to end, were delightful, risqué puffs of froth. Their main themes were sex and money, with the former a charming game played by those who had ample supplies of the latter. Always involved were fairy-tale characters: debonair, lavishly uniformed guardsmen with roving eyes who became the love targets of queens and princesses from small (many of them imaginary) European countries.

That such characters and locales were selected for the plot was no accident. Lubitsch understood that Americans liked sex and money, but he understood just as well that, should his pictures be given an American setting, the bluenose side of the American character might well surface with annoyance and demand a retribution at the film's end that simply wouldn't work in a happy motion picture. He was dead right. Coming out of Hollywood at the time was a string of sexually accented pictures, and not a few scandals. This eventually led to a moviegoers' revolt and the establishment of the ridiculously strict Will Hays Motion Picture Production Code in 1930.

The Marriage Circle was a marital comedy of errors that was ideally suited to the Lubitsch Touch. It took place in pre-World War I Vienna and told of a bachelor's experiences with two married couples – one happily married and the other miserable. The film starred Florence Vidor, Monte Blue, Marie Prevost, Creighton Hale and Adolphe Menjou, but it didn't make money, although it became a favorite of Charlie Chaplin and Alfred Hitchcock, who appreciated Lubitsch's techniques and skills.

Rin-Tin-Tin was the big star at Warners, but slowly catching up to him was the young John Barrymore. He first appeared with Mary Astor in *Beau Brummell* (1924), which was so successful that the studio signed him to a long term contract at $76,250 per movie, as long as the films were completed in six weeks. For every week of overtime, he was to be paid $6625. In addition, he had the right to approve his leading lady and the studio paid for a four-room suite for him at the Ambassador Hotel, as well as paying for all his meals and the cost of a chauffer-driven limousine.

Above: *Johnny Hines gets his victory kiss from Molly Malone as Margaret Seddon and Wyndham Standing look on in* Little Johnny Jones.
Opposite: *Louise Fazenda (pointing) gives advice to Hope Hampton (standing) in* The Gold Diggers *(1923).*

Right: *Irene Rich in a tender scene with John Barrymore –* Beau Brummell *(1924).*

Left: *Patsy Ruth Miller waves goodbye to Clive Brook in* Why Girls Go Back Home *(1926).*
Opposite: *The peglegged Captain Abab (John Barrymore) in pain in* The Sea Beast *(1926) – a heavily rewritten film version of Herman Melville's great novel,* Moby Dick.

Below: *May McAvoy was Lady Windermere and Ronald Colman was Lord Darlington in the screen adaptation of Oscar Wilde's play,* Lady Windermere's Fan *(1925).*

Beau Brummell (1924) told the story of a Regency gentleman who becomes the friend of the Prince of Wales, but dies penniless because of his arrogance. Such a part fit Barrymore to a T, and the 17-year-old Astor was so beautiful as Lady Margery Alvanly that Barrymore said that her stunning appearance made him feel faint. The movie was a hit and everyone in the audiences applauded, except for a few angry lip-readers who were able to tell that while the silent cameras were photographing him, Barrymore was uttering obscenities to Willard Louis, who played the Prince of Wales.

Broadway After Dark (1924) was Adolphe Menjou's first starring hit. Menjou, having been hurt in an unhappy love affair, leaves the glitter of Broadway to live in a theatrical boarding house. Also in the cast were Anna Q Nilsson and a 24-year-old Norma Shearer.

Rin-Tin-Tin came back in *Find Your Man* (1924), in which his master (Eric St Clair) is falsely accused of murder. Naturally, Rinty tracks down the murderer, and almost everyone lives happily ever after. The most important thing about this film was that it was written in four days by a new Warner Bros. employee – 22-year-old Darryl F Zanuck.

Another Lubitsch film of 1924 was *Three Women*. Pauline Frederick was a widow, May McAvoy was her daughter and Marie Prevost was the mistress of a roué (Lew Cody). Cody is trying to have affairs with all three of them. The movie was a critical success but a box office failure.

Kiss Me Again (1925) was another Lubitsch tale of infidelity. Marie Prevost is bored with her husband, Monte Blue, and indulges in some hanky-panky with her pianist lover, John Roche. In the end the husband wins out. Thanks to Lubitsch's skill, the critics called it 'one of the most penetrating, witty and intelligent studies of the mechanics of romantic love ever filmed.'

Ernst Lubitsch's other film in 1925 was *Lady Windermere's Fan*, which, although a silent movie, managed to capture the wit of Oscar Wilde's play. Lubitsch said that he had substituted 'visual epigrams' for Wilde's verbal ones. He was also

helped by the wonderful cast that included Irene Rich, May McAvoy, Bert Lytell and the 34-year-old Ronald Colman.

A Lost Lady (1925) was based on Willa Cather's novel of the same name and starred Irene Rich. It told of a spoiled wife who is bored by her older husband but can't figure out what she wants out of life. So she deserts her husband in order to find herself.

Warners made a big mistake in trying to capitalize on the popularity of Charlie Chaplin by starring his brother Sydney in *The Man on the Box* (1925). Sydney Chaplin strained for his laughs – something that his brother never would have done – disguising himself as a parlor maid and telling a male apache dancer that he was mistreating his partner.

John Barrymore kept Warners solvent in 1926 with two feature films, *The Sea Beast* and *Don Juan*. *The Sea Beast* was an adaptation of Herman Melville's novel, *Moby Dick*, but it was so rewritten that it bore practically no resemblance to the original. Barrymore, however, was great. He had asked the studio to star him as Captain Ahab because, as he put it, he was 'tired of playing so many scented, be-puffed, bewigged and ringletted characters.' The search for the great white

whale stayed in the picture, but love interest and a happy ending were added. Priscilla Bonner was supposed to be Ahab's love, but Barrymore asked for Mary Astor. Astor was not available, so Barrymore settled for an unknown, Dolores Costello. Bonner sued the studio for breach of contract, and the case was settled out of court. The highlights of this $800,000 epic were the steamy clinches between Barrymore and Costello. Apparently there was a chemistry there, because they were later married.

Barrymore proved himself to be a valid rival of Douglas Fairbanks Sr in *Don Juan* (1926), Warner's first full-length attempt at using the new Vitaphone sound. The picture opened at the Manhattan Opera House in New York City on 6 August 1926. The program began with some short subjects with sound, featuring musical stars like violinist Mischa Elman and tenor Giovanni Martinelli, followed by the feature film, which had no dialogue, but did have a sound track with music and sound effects. Darryl F Zanuck, by this time the production chief at Warners, hired the New York Philharmonic to record the background music for the picture. A silent version was also made for theaters that did not have sound equipment.

Barrymore, swinging on vines, leaping off balconies, swimming an icy river and jumping off the tops of stairs, was a swashbuckling marvel. The various women he courted in the film received 191 kisses, according to a press agent. Getting their shares of the lovemaking were Mary Astor, Estelle Taylor, Myrna Loy, Phyllis Haver and June Marlowe. Warner Oland played Cesare Borgia.

So This Is Paris (1926) was the only money-making film that Lubitsch ever made for Warners. It was, of course, another infidelity romp concerning two married couples. But it was witty, elegant, satirical and fun. The movie starred Monte Blue, Patsy Ruth Miller, Lilyan Tashman and Myrna Loy.

Why Girls Go Back Home (1926) was a real winner – a comedy about an actor who lets success on Broadway go to his head and ignores his former girl friend when she arrives in New York to become an actress. She is successful, too, and lowers the boom on her former love. It starred Clive Brook (a subtitle called him 'Broadway's newest pain'), Patsy Ruth Miller and Myrna Loy.

23

One of 1926's anomalies was *Private Izzy Murphy*, whose plot obviously was stolen from the long-running Broadway stage hit *Abie's Irish Rose*. It was in this film that George Jessel made his Hollywood debut. The story was about a Roman Catholic girl and a Jewish boy, but she doesn't know he is Jewish because he has changed his name to Isadore Patrick Murphy (why he kept the Isadore was not explained). He enlists in the Army and confesses his duplicity by mail from France. But when he returns he finds that the girl still loves him, and they decide to get married. This tear-jerker also starred Patsy Ruth Miller and the never-to-be-forgotten Gustav von Seyffertitz.

Darryl F Zanuck adapted Charles E Balney's play *Across the Pacific* (1926), which starred Monte Blue as a spy sent to the Philippines to track down a rebel leader, and Myrna Loy as a half-caste (a typical role for her at the time).

Zanuck also wrote a screwball comedy under the pen name of Gregory Rogers called *Three Weeks in Paris* (1926), which had as successful an 'it was all a dream' ending as anything this side of *The Wizard of Oz*. Matt Moore played a man who is forced to leave his wife (Dorothy Devore) on their wedding night. He goes to Paris, is involved in a duel,

Above: *Every army comedy has to have slapstick scenes of a confrontation of a private with his overbearing sergeant. Here are George Jessel (left) and Edgar Kennedy in* Private Izzy Murphy *(1926).*
Left: *Rin-Tin-Tin holds a drifter captive while waiting for his master in* While London Sleeps *(1926).*

Opposite: *Al Jolson in his patented pose singing 'Mammy' in* The Jazz Singer *(1927). The plot of the film wasn't much, but Jolson's overwhelming stage personality shone through.*

and is thought to be dead when the steamship on which he is supposed to return to the United States sinks. But it was a dream, and the two turn out to be a happy, albeit dull, married couple.

Rin-Tin-Tin was still big at the box office in 1926. A typical film of his, *Hero of the Big Snows*, involved his delivery of a message to his master. A storm had caused a tree to fall on a young girl, who cannot therefore get to a doctor to be treated for her illness. But in *While London Sleeps* (also 1926), Rinty went to the city. This was the story of a murderer who prowls the streets of London with his pet monster and his dog (Rin-Tin-Tin). Of course Rinty befriends the daughter of Inspector Burke of Scotland Yard, who catches the killer.

Occasionally Monte Blue could turn in a good comedy performance. In *Wolf's Clothing* (1927) he played a subway

station guard. Told he could have New Year's Eve off – his first night off in three years – he starts to go on the town, but is knocked down by a car. His hallucinations make up the best part of the film, one of them being that he has become doll-sized. That was all right, because so has Patsy Ruth Miller.

Rin-Tin-Tin returned to the country in *Hills of Kentucky* (1927), saving the heroine from dying in a fall over a cataract. He also had to cope with Rin-Tin-Tin Jr while tracking down the villain.

The movie version of David Belasco's play, *The Heart of Maryland* (1927), starred Dolores Costello as a Southerner and Jason Robards Sr as a Union man. Because this took place during the Civil War, there were problems of their getting together. But when the South surrendered, the romance could begin again.

Sydney Chaplin co-starred with a pride of lions, a chimpanzee, a leopard, a dog and Ruth Hall in *The Missing Link* (1927). He played the part of a poor (financially and talent-wise) poet who becomes a big game hunter searching for the missing link that will explain how apes evolved into humans. The problem was that he hated and feared animals, which led to some rather funny situations out in the wild.

Abbé Prevost's classic, *Manon Lescaut*, was redone in 1927 and retitled *When a Man Loves*, starring John Barrymore as des Grieux and Dolores Costello as Manon. It had a Vitaphone orchestral accompaniment, just as *Don Juan* had had. The plot, somewhat altered, involves a swashbuckler who escapes from a French prison ship, taking Manon with him, and it gave Barrymore another chance to chew the scenery. It also starred Warner Oland at his meanest as Manon's brother.

George Jessel returned with another Izzy Murphy film, *Sailor Izzy Murphy* (1927). This time he was a perfume salesman who falls in love with the picture of the woman on the perfume bottles. He learns that she is the daughter of the perfume company's president, finds her on a yacht, and also finds that there is a lunatic on the boat who is trying to kill the perfume manufacturer because the man has killed so many

flowers in making his product. Izzy captures the lunatic and the girl falls in love with him.

Warners' previous experiment with sound, *Don Juan*, had its orchestral gimmick, but it hadn't worked. The music seemed to be coming from behind the screen rather than from the orchestra pit, but that wasn't the real problem. Theater owners resisted buying the expensive equipment necessary for that little innovation. So for a year after *Don Juan*, only a few theaters had the equipment and all they had to show were those 'Vitaphone Shorts.'

Then came *The Jazz Singer* (1927).

Al Jolson was an established star on Broadway and he asked a lot of money for this experimental film. The Warner Brothers didn't have all that much money, so they offered him stock in their company instead. Had Jolson accepted, he would have received a fortune, but he refused, and the Warner Brothers somehow got enough money together to hire him.

The Jazz Singer was not really the first musical, or the first sound motion picture – it was a melodrama that highlighted seven songs sung by Jolson, plus a few lines of dialogue that he reputedly ad-libbed on the set and that were allowed to

remain. Those included his patented 'You ain't heard nothin' yet' and a speech to his screen mother, played by Eugenie Besserer.

But the songs were sensational. Among them were such Jolson trademarks as 'Toot Toot Tootsie Goodbye' and 'Mammy,' plus 'My Gal Sal,' 'Waiting for the Robert E Lee,' 'Dirty Hands, Dirty Face,' 'Mother, I Still Have You' and the reverent 'Kol Nidre,' sung in synagogues on the Day of Atonement. 'Mother, I Still Have You' was the first song ever written especially for use in a film.

The movie was not great. It was a mediocre picture with a shopworn story. Running for 88 minutes, it told the tale of young Jakie Rabinowitz (Jolson) who alienated his father (played by Warner Oland, who went on to play the title roles in 16 Charlie Chan movies) by abandoning a future as a cantor and following a career in jazz singing that eventually took him to stardom. Sam Warner, who was primarily responsible for the movie and this revolution in film-making, died under the pressure, just 24 hours before the grand opening.

The Jazz Singer opened on Friday night, 6 October 1927 and the movies were never to be the same. The audience was enchanted. There were bursts of applause after every number, and a standing ovation at the end of the film. It was a Warner Bros. triumph. They had given birth to the movie musical and convinced other producers that sound was here to stay – all in one evening. The next day they took out an ad in *The New York Times*:

> We apologize to the thousands who were turned away from last night's premiere. If the WARNER THEATER were as large as Madison Square Garden, we still would not have been able to accommodate the crowds that clamored for admission. There will be two performances daily at 2:45 & 8:45, and we respectfully suggest that you purchase tickets well in advance.

The revolution had happened. Manufacturers of the sound equipment were swamped with orders from exhibitors. By the end of the year even the most confirmed skeptics realized that any sound film was attracting huge crowds to any theater that showed it. By the spring of 1928, the worst sound film would outdraw the best silent movie in any town.

Of course there were problems with the new sound systems. Early recording equipment was so sensitive that it even picked up sounds made by fabrics. Therefore taffeta could not be used at all, and petticoats had to be made of felt and wool rather than silk. Shoes had to be soled with felt or rubber. The Vitaphone camera had to be enclosed in a soundproof booth so that the whirring of the camera itself would not be recorded. And it was hot in the booth. Without air conditioning, the temperature inside would rise to the point where cameramen could stay inside for only a few minutes at a time.

By the middle of 1928, all the Hollywood studios had to face three new problems with the sound film. They had to re-equip with sound devices. They had to figure out what to do with their backstock of silent films. They had to do something with their contract actors and actresses whose voices were not up to the primitive recording equipment of the day.

Panic was the order of the times, and many of the pictures suffered. Gone was the free-flowing action and continuity of the silent movie. In was a static, stagelike technique caused by the fact that the microphone was immovable and all action had to be centered around the spot where the mike was.

Cameras, in their booths, could no longer be moved around freely. The director could no longer give audible suggestions as a scene was being photographed.

But Warner Bros. was not worried. They had a jump on the other studios in this sound revolution, and they knew it. Almost immediately they released *Tenderloin* (1928), which was the first all-talking picture in which the characters spoke their own lines. Dolores Costello played a dancer who was accused of stealing $50,000, and that meant that both the police and the underworld were after her. Conrad Nagel costarred in the part of a gangster.

The Lion and the Mouse (1928) was not an important picture, but a rather silly one about a powerful financier (Lionel Barrymore) who is conquered by a mousey girl (May McAvoy). The important thing about the film was that it established as fact the idea that some actors could not act and talk at the same time. The movie had 31 minutes of dialogue, and Barrymore was magnificent, but he was the only one in the film who delivered.

Lights of New York (1928) was a terrible picture, but a

landmark all the same. It was hokey – telling the story of a country boy who is bilked by wicked Broadway characters. Still, it was an all-talkie, starring Helene Costello, Cullen Landis, Eugene Pallette and Mary Carr, and the film, which had cost $75,000 to make, earned $2,000,000, although the sound reproduction was wretched.

The first Warner Vitaphone picture without a single sub-title was *The Terror* (1928), which frightened the American audiences but gave British audiences a case of the giggles. Although it starred May McAvoy, Louise Fazenda and Edward Everett Horton, it took place in a British hotel, where an organ-playing homicidal maniac prowled the halls. The sound track also contained sound effects such as rain, thunder, creaking floorboards and organ recitals. Some unkind critics suggested that McAvoy's squeaky voice was just another sound effect.

The Night Watch (1928) was an important film only in the respect that it probably gave birth to a genre that was later to become a fascinating Hollywood staple in such movies as *The Court-Martial of Billy Mitchell* (1955), *The Caine Mutiny* (1954) and *Paths of Glory* (1957). It was a World War I drama that began in a courtroom where a captain of a war ship is accused of shooting one of his officers. Then came the flash-backs concerning what had happened. The picture starred Paul Lukas as the captain and Billie Dove as his wife.

Al Jolson returned to the screen in 1928 in *The Singing Fool*. The plot was so melodramatic that the theaters must have been awash in tears – of either sympathy or laughter. It was a dismal tear-jerker about a brash entertainer who comes to his senses when his little boy dies, memorable only because Jolson sang 'Sonny Boy' in it.

Dancing Vienna (1929) was a paean to the waltz. The lavish film opened with a visit to heaven by the Emperor Franz Josef of Austria. It seems that he is worried about the incursions that jazz music has been making on the music of the waltz, and he asks Mozart, Offenbach and Johann Strauss if they can do something about it. They decide to cooperate. The rest of the movie concerned a cabaret singer who wins the love of the son of a rich American. Lya Mara was the girl and Ben Lyon was the boy.

Richard Barthelmess, the star of *Weary River* (1929), played a crook who is sent to prison when one of his rivals rats on him. While he is in jail, he discovers he can sing and takes on the job of leading the convicts' band – singing the title song over and over until the audience was sick of it. The only memorable thing about the picture was that it was one of the first Warner Bros. pictures to use a prison as a setting – a harbinger of the many prison pictures to come from the studio.

It took Hollywood a couple of years after the advent of sound to realize that the Broadway musical would be ideal for sound films, but when the idea dawned, movie moguls grabbed the rights to stage musical comedies with a ven-geance. And Warner Bros. was in the vanguard of the movement. One of the first properties to appear on the screen was *The Desert Song* (1929), adapted from the stage show of the same name, first produced in 1926 with lyrics by Otto Harbach and Oscar Hammerstein II and music by Sigmund Romberg. *The Desert Song* was an unusual musical for the time because it had a modern setting – the 1925 revolt of the Riffs against the French Protectorate in Morocco.

Opposite: *May McAvoy is abducted by a hooded stranger in* The Terror *(1928).*

Above: *Lya Mara as the cabaret entertainer in love with Ben Lyon in* Dancing Vienna *(1929).*

The plot concerned Margot, a gullible French girl who is unaware that her boy friend, Pierre Birabeau, the somewhat wimpy son of the French governor, is also 'the Red Shadow' – the leader of the Riffs. Being the typical swashbuckler heroine, she doesn't recognize him even when he tries, as the Red Shadow, to lure her into the desert by singing what became the title song, also known as 'Blue Heaven.' Margot does go into the desert, but spurns the Red Shadow. When he returns to her tent as Pierre, Margot says that she loves the Red Shadow. It takes her until the end of the movie to realize that the two men are one and the same.

The film starring John Boles, Carlotta King and Myrna Loy, was shot in a primitive two-color Technicolor process, but

Above: *The lovely Corinne Griffith played Lady Emma Hamilton and Victor Varconi was Lord Nelson in* The Divine Lady *(1929).*

retained most of the original Broadway score. In addition to the title song, there were the 'Riff Song,' the 'French Marching Song,' 'Then You Will Know,' 'Song of the Brass Key,' 'Sabre Song,' 'Romance,' 'One Alone,' 'One Flower' and 'My Little Castagnette.'

The Divine Lady (1929) told the story of Lord Nelson and Emma Hamilton, and starred Victor Varconi and Corinne Griffith, with Marie Dressler as Emma's mother. It was basically a silent with sound effects, but it did have a theme song, 'Lady Divine.'

One of the most ambitious films of 1929 was Warners' *Noah's Ark*. It was a part talkie that ran for the then unheard of time of two hours and 15 minutes, and told the Biblical story with the addition of a parallel World War I romance. It is fair to say that the special effects scenes of the flood stole the show. But, unfortunately, several extras drowned during the shooting. Starring were Dolores Costello as Miriam, Noah Beery Sr as King Nephilim, Guinn 'Big Boy' Williams as Ham, Paul McAllister as Noah, Malcolm Waite as Shem, Myrna Loy as a slave girl and Louise Fazenda as a tavern maid.

Warner Bros. tried another musical – *Broadway Babies* (1929) – starring Alice White, Charles Delaney and Fred Kohler, but it was only a mild success. Kohler tries to steal

White from Delaney, but is shot by a gangster with an air gun. The long-forgotten musical score included 'Wishing and Waiting for Love,' 'Jig Jig Jigaloo' and 'Broadway Baby Doll.'

On With the Show (1929) was billed as 'the first 100 percent natural color all singing production.' It starred the beautiful Betty Compson, whose singing voice was dubbed and for whom a professional dancer had to be substituted in the long shots. The movie was memorable only in the fact that Joe E Brown made his Warner Bros. debut in it. Arthur Lake (later to become Dagwood Bumstead in the *Blondie* movie series) and Sally O'Neil also contributed to the film. Ethel Waters did, however, perk up the picture when she appeared to sing 'Am I Blue?' and 'Birmingham Bertha.'

'The Last of the Red-Hot Mommas,' Sophie Tucker, was wonderful in *Honky Tonk* (1929), playing the part of a mother who sacrifices everything so that her daughter can get an education. Of course, à la Stella Dallas, the girl won't have anything to do with her mother when she finds out that Sophie Tucker is a lowly night club entertainer. The lack of a decent plot was offset by Tucker's singing 'Some of These Days,' among other hits.

Gold Diggers of Broadway (1929) was yet another adaptation of the Avery Hopwood play *The Gold Diggers*. Again, it was the same old story of three girls and their pursuit of wealthy sugar daddies. The girls were Nancy Welford, Ann Pennington and Winnie Lightner, and others in the cast were

Above: *The 1929 film version of* The Desert Song *spared no expense in hiring actors and dancers and designing costumes and sets.*

Right: *John Boles, as the Red Shadow, evidently is saying 'They went thataway' in* The Desert Song *(1929).*

Conway Tearle, Lilyan Tashman, William Bakewell and Nick Lukas. The plot was terrible, despite the ads' promise that the movie was 'a profuse procession of revue spectacle scenes in amazing settings . . . superbly staged chorus dancing numbers . . . a story that had New York gasping for one solid year.' The picture was shot in the two-color Technicolor process of the time, and the Al Dubin-Joe Burke score was fine, featuring 'Tiptoe Through the Tulips' and 'Painting the Clouds with Sunshine.'

Disraeli (1929) marked the sound film debut of George Arliss, who was 61 years old at the time. Billed as *Mr* George Arliss, the respected actor played the British Prime Minister again, emoting histrionically and using dated silent film acting techniques. This was a holdover from 1921, when he had appeared in a silent version of the same story. The screenplay concentrated on Disraeli's attempts to thwart the Russians and buy the Suez Canal, with a little fictional matchmaking thrown in.

The Forward Pass (1929) was notable only in that it starred Douglas Fairbanks Jr and Loretta Young. Of course Fairbanks wins the game and the girl, while songs such as 'One Minute of Heaven,' 'I Gotta Have You' and 'H'lo Baby' are being sung.

Al Jolson was paid one half million dollars for making *Say It With Songs* (1929). It was a formula picture, having a mournful dirge, 'Little Pal,' that was reminiscent of 'Sonny

Boy.' Jolson played a radio singer who kills a man for flirting with his wife. Jolson is sent to jail and the picture flopped.

Cole Porter's Broadway musical comedy *Paris* was the story of a mother who doesn't want her son to marry a chorus girl and takes him off to Paris. Even though the stage musical had run for a stunning 195 performances, Warners was afraid the sophisticated Porter songs would ruin the movie's chances of success. So an all new score by Al Bryan and Ed Ward including 'Crystal Girl,' 'Miss Wonderful,' 'Paris,' 'I Wonder What Is Really on His Mind.' 'I'm a Little Negative,' 'Somebody Might Like You' and 'My Lover' ('Master of My Heart') was used in the film. Starring in the roles they introduced on Broadway were Irene Bordoni (as the chorus girl) and Jack Buchanan. Also in the cast were Jason Robards Sr, as the son, and ZaSu Pitts. Warner Bros. tried everything – Vitaphone sound and two-color Technicolor sequences – but the movie was a failure. It needed Cole Porter.

The Show of Shows (1929) was a mishmash publicized as 'A connoisseur's collection of the supreme examples of almost every form of stage and screen entertainment.' Actually, it was an all-star film revue similar to ones produced by other studios, featuring such diverse Warners' talents as Beatrice Lillie, Douglas Fairbanks Jr, Loretta Young, Winnie Lightner, Chester Morris and Harriette Lake. Ms Lake was a sparkling bit player who, four years later, attained star status under her new name, Ann Sothern.

Warner Bros. ended the decade with a remake of a previous 1923 hit, the sound version of *Little Johnny Jones* (1929) which featured Eddie Buzzell in the title role. All but two of the George M Cohan songs had been removed ('Give My Regards to Broadway' and 'Yankee Doodle Boy'). Added songs included 'Painting the Clouds with Sunshine' by Al Dubin and Joe Burke, 'Straight, Place and Show' by Herman Ruby and M K Jerome, 'Go Find Somebody in Love' by Herb Magidson and Michael Cleary and 'My Paradise' by Magidson and James Cavanaugh.

The 1920s had come to a triumphant end, but much more was to come from Warner Bros. in the next decade.

Above: *Again, Warner Bros. spared very little expense in the production numbers of* Gold Diggers of Broadway *(1929).*
Opposite: *Alice White (at the door), as the virginal chorus girl, listens to strange noises as Sally Eilers and Marion Byron express curiosity in* Broadway Babies *(1929).*

Right: *George Arliss, age 61, made his sound picture debut as* Disraeli *(1929). Here he is (right), introducing a very young Joan Bennett (aged 19) to the love of her life.*

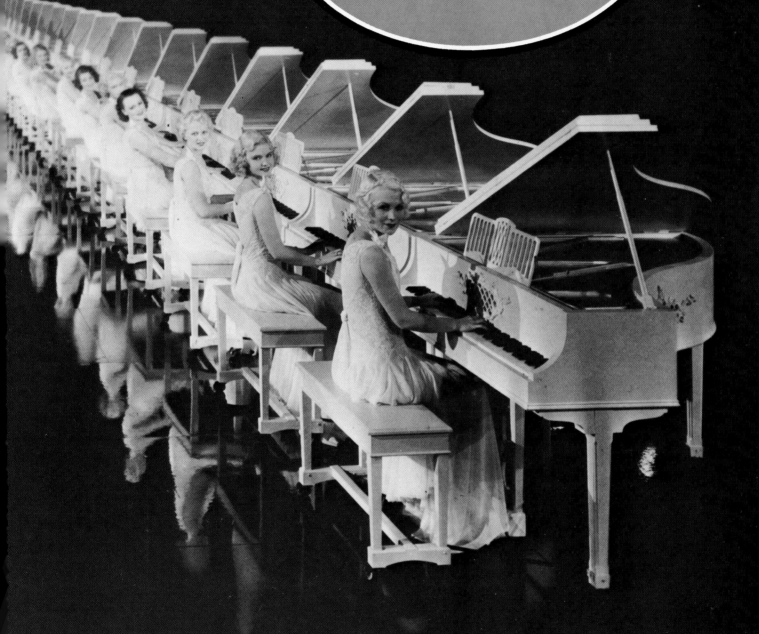

THE THIRTIES

IN THE EARLY 1930S America found itself in the depths of the Great Depression – a time when almost everyone had to think twice before paying the price of a ticket to a movie theater. In 1929, 110 million people paid admission to motion picture palaces. The very next year, the total number of motion picture customers dropped to 50 million. Warner Bros. profits went from 14 million dollars in 1929 to seven million dollars in 1930, and then the studio lost money in 1931 – seven million dollars. Faced with losses, it was Darryl F Zanuck who insisted that Warners switch to realistic films, reflecting the headlines of the day and a concern for society's losers.

It was at this time that Warners became known as 'the working man's studio.' Prohibition saw the rise of the gangster, and Warner Bros. gave the public gangster films. Even the musicals of the studio were realistic. *Forty-Second Street* (1933) was not a frothy fantasy, but hard-hitting and at times harsh. The studio also became adept at making prison movies and women's films.

By 1930 Warner Bros. was a real Hollywood power, owning 51 subsidiary companies, employing 18,500 people and maintaining 525 theaters in 188 cities. That year, George Arliss won an Oscar for his work in *Disraeli*.

But by 1931 the studio was hurting financially, and had to lay off 900 employees and give salary cuts of between 20 and 30 percent. That year also saw the beginning of what came to be known as the Warner Bros. Stock Company, featuring Bette Davis, James Cagney, Barbara Stanwyck, Edward G Robinson, Joan Blondell, Loretta Young, Mary Astor and Douglas Fairbanks Jr.

By 1932 Jack Warner was disgusted by the way some of his stars were behaving, so he and Zanuck issued a joint proclamation that said that no artist under contract would have any say about any aspect of a film's production. James Cagney, for the second time in the decade, was dissatisfied with his $1000 per week contract and quit the studio. After arbitration, he returned at a salary of $1750 per week at a time when Joan Blondell was earning a mere $250. Also in 1932, Rin-Tin-Tin died at the age of 16, after earning more than $5,000,000 for his owner, Leland Duncan. Despite all the economy measures of that year and the previous one, the studio lost another 14 million dollars.

The Depression marched on in 1933. That spring all Warner Bros. employees had to take a 50 percent pay reduction for a period of eight weeks. Still the studio lost more than six million dollars that year. Meantime, Twentieth Century Pictures merged with Fox, becoming Twentieth Century-Fox, and they were able to steal Darryl F Zanuck (who was making $5000 per week) from Warners. Zanuck was to serve as head of production at Twentieth for the next 25 years.

A sidelight in Warner Bros. history in 1934 was the banning of all of their films by the government of Poland. The Polish Minister of the Interior felt that the Warner crime movies showed Polish gangsters as being vicious. Toward the end of the year there was a tremendous fire in the studio which took the life of Warners' fire chief and did hundreds of thousands of dollars worth of damage, plus the destruction of irreplaceable early Vitagraph, Warner Bros. and First National Prints. But losses were cut to two and a half million dollars, and William Randolph Hearst's film company, Cosmopolitan Productions, switched its distribution connection from MGM to Warners and moved to Burbank.

The following November (1935), Benjamin Warner died in Youngstown while visiting one of his daughters. Added to the Warner Brothers Stock Company in 1935 were such stars as Margaret Lindsay, Glenda Farrell, Hugh Herbert, Guy Kibbee, George Brent, Claire Dodd, Hobart Cavanaugh and Barton MacLane. The studio finally was out of the red, earning over one half million dollars, and Bette Davis won her first Oscar for *Dangerous*. Warners also collected an Oscar for best song in a motion picture – 'Lullaby of Broadway' from *Gold Diggers of 1935* by Harry Warren and Al Dubin.

By 1936 more people found that they could afford an occasional trip to a movie theater and attendance climbed to 85 million, nationally. But part of the gain was due to double and triple features and such gimmicks as Bank Night and Dish Night. Warner profits were up to over three million dollars, and the studio had enough money to start making costume movies – beginning a long line of films for which they would become famous. Two Warner Bros. stars won Academy Awards in 1936 – Paul Muni was best actor in *The Story of Louis Pasteur* and Gale Sondergaard was best supporting actress for *Anthony Adverse*.

Warners finally won an Oscar for the best film of the year – *The Life of Emile Zola* – in 1937. For the same movie, Joseph Schildkraut won the Academy Award as best supporting actor. *Zola* was also named as the best picture of the year by the New York film critics, who gave an award to Paul Muni as best actor. And profits had climbed to almost six million dollars.

The studio lost about two million dollars in 1938, probably because they spent money on 51 feature films that year. But several of the movies were monumental. *Jezebel* won two Oscars – Bette Davis as best actress and Fay Bainter as best supporting actress – and *The Adventures of Robin Hood* won three – for art director Carl Jules Weyl, editor Ralph Dawson and film score composer Erich Wolfgang Korngold.

Salaries were becoming inflated at Warner Bros. in 1939. Cagney was earning $12,500 per week; Paul Muni $11,500; Edward G Robinson $8000; Claude Rains $6000; George Raft $5000; Bette Davis $4000; Pat O'Brien $4000; Frank McHugh $1600; John Garfield $1500; Olivia de Havilland $1250, while younger players earned much less, Priscilla Lane $75; Ann Sheridan $500 and Jane Wyman $200. Still, the company was back in the black again with a profit of almost two million dollars.

The 1930s started out with a bang when Warner Bros. released *Sally* (1930). Marilyn Miller, the legendary musical comedy actress, had starred in the Broadway musical of 1920. *Sally* had a book by Guy Bolton, and the lyrics by Clifford Grey and Buddy de Sylva were set to music by Jerome Kern. Additional ballet music was by Victor Herbert.

As usual for musicals, the story wasn't much. A former Balkan grand duke exiled by a revolution, Connie, becomes a waiter at the Elm Tree Inn. He takes a little dishwasher, Sally (Miller), under his wing and helps her crash a huge party at the Long Island estate of wealthy Otis Hooper, as a Russian dancer. Her performance there is the beginning of a dancing career that leads to the Ziegfeld Follies. She then meets and marries wealthy Blair Farquar and lives happily ever after.

Warner Bros. lured Marilyn Miller to Hollywood to make the screen version of *Sally* (1930), and they spared no expense with the film, lavishing a fortune in hopes of repeating its Broadway success. According to the film's publicity flacks, Sally was helped on her way to Broadway by

'150 beauties in the largest indoor scene ever photographed in color . . . 36 Albertina Rasch girls who dance more perfectly than other choruses can clog . . . an orchestra of 110 to play the song hits that *Sally* made famous, and many new numbers added for the screen production.' Also in the cast were Joe E Brown, the comedian with the giant mouth; Ford Sterling, one of the leading Keystone Kops; and Pert Kelton, who would finally gain recognition as a comedienne 28 years later as Mrs Paroo in *The Music Man* (1957).

The film retained three of the original Broadway songs – 'Look for the Silver Lining,' 'Wild Rose' and 'Sally.' Added were some other songs by Al Dubin and Joe Burke – 'Walking Off Those Balkan Blues,' 'After Business Hours' ('That Certain Business Begins'), 'All I want to Do Do Do Is Dance,' 'If I'm Dreaming Don't Wake Me Up Too Soon' and 'What Will I Do Without You?'

Another Warner Bros. musical of 1930 was *Song of the West*, which was based on an unsuccessful show of 1928, *Rainbow*. The plot involved a US Army Scout who breaks out of the prison where he is being held on a murder charge, joins the Gold Rush of 1849 and finds happiness. The show had traces of what later became *Oklahoma!* and *Paint Your Wagon*. Perhaps when Oscar Hammerstein II became so enthusiastic about *Oklahoma!*, he knew what had gone

wrong with the production of *Rainbow* which ran a mere 30 performances on Broadway, despite music by Vincent Youmans and a book and lyrics by Hammerstein, Laurence Stallings and Edward Eliscu.

The stars of *Song Of The West* were John Boles and Vivienne Segal, who were hindered by poor sound recording, a bad script by Harvey Thew and lazy direction by Ray Enright. Comic relief was added by Joe E Brown playing a guitar.

One of the big Broadway hits of 1925 had been *No, No, Nanette*, with a book by Otto Harbach, lyrics by Irving Caesar and Otto Harbach and music by Vincent Youmans. It ran for 321 performances.

As usual, there wasn't much of a plot. On a holiday in Atlantic City, Billy Early, a Bible publisher, finds three girls who need his help: Betty from Boston, Flora from San Francisco and Winnie from Washington. Meanwhile, the lawyer, Jimmy Smith, is chasing Billy's daughter Nanette. She disappears from the hotel for a night and Tom, her fiancee, is righteously concerned. Everything turns out all right when Billy's wife pay off the girls and Tom forgives Nanette.

Warner Bros. adapted this froth for the screen in their version of *No, No, Nanette* (1930), which was shot in the primitive Technicolor of the time. The film starred Bernice Claire as Nanette, and the cast included Alexander Gray, Lilyan Tashman, Zasu Pitts, Louise Fazenda and Lucien Littlefield. In addition to the title song, 'Tea For Two' and 'I Want to Be Happy,' by Youmans and Caesar, the movie featured

'Dance of the Wooden Shoes' by Ned Washington, Herb Magidson and Michael Cleary, 'As Long As I'm With You' by Grant Clarke and Harry Akst and 'King of the Air' and 'Dancing to Heaven' by Al Bryan and Ed Ward.

A Notorious Affair (1930) was one of Warners' early women's pictures. Billie Dove played a socialite who loses her position in society by marrying Basil Rathbone, a violinist. But Rathbone is caught having an affair with Kay Francis. Naturally Dove leaves him, only to return to nurse him back to health after he falls ill. There wasn't a dry eye in the house.

When the sporting comedy *Hold Everything* appeared as a Warner Bros. movie in 1930, it had been rewritten as a vehicle for Joe E Brown, who played Gink Shiner (get it?), the boxer. Winnie Lightner played his girl friend, and real life light heavyweight champion Georges Charpentier guest starred as the heavyweight champion Georges LaVerne. Unfortunately the original score by Buddy de Sylva, Ray Henderson and Lew Brown was scrapped and a new one written by Al Dubin and Joe Burke that included such forgettables as 'Take It on the Chin,' 'When Little Red Roses Get the Blues for You,' 'Sing a Little Theme Song,' 'Physically Fit,' 'Girls We Remember,' 'All Alone Together' and 'Isn't This a Cockeyed World?'

In 1930, Warner Bros. was unable to resist the idea of filming an operetta, and *Song of the Flame* based on the 1925 Broadway show with music by George Gershwin and Herbert Stothart, and book and lyrics by Otto Harbach and Oscar

Hammerstein II, was released that year. Bernice Claire played the part of a peasant girl known as 'The Flame,' who causes a Russian revolution by singing 'Song of the Flame.' A sub-plot involved her love affair with a Russian Prince (Alexander Gray) whose life she saves by agreeing to the sexual demands of an evil peasant revolutionary (Noah Beery Sr, singing, no less). Shot in Technicolor, the production experimented with the use of a wide screen at one point, but the story was sappy and the direction unremarkable.

The studio kept two of the original songs from the stage musical – 'The Cossack Love Song' and 'Song of the Flame' by Hammerstein, Stothart, Gershwin and Harbach. Other numbers were 'Petrograd,' 'Liberty Song,' 'The Goose Hangs High,' 'Passing Fancy' and 'One Little Drink' by Grant Clarke, Harry Akst and Ed Ward, and 'When Love Calls' by Ed Ward.

Mammy (1930) was a hit and it proved that the name Al Jolson was still a magic one. Jolson played an endman in a traveling minstrel show, and the addition of Irving Berlin songs made the show a smash hit. Some of the scenes were shot in color, a technique that had become quite common.

Erich von Stroheim, once known as a director, saved the melodrama *Three Faces East* (1930) from becoming a disaster. His forceful performance as a German spy masquerading as the butler of the First Lord of the British Admiralty was so compelling that audiences forgot the thinness of the plot line.

Warner Bros. began its foray into war films with *The Dawn Patrol* (1930). Set in the France of 1915, it dealt with a

Right: *Alexander Gray and Bernice Claire (as The Flame) in an amorous moment in* Song of the Flame *(1930).*
Left: *Bernice Claire and Alexander Gray ('King of the Air') together again in* No, No, Nanette *(1930).*

Below: *Al Jolson in* Mammy *(1930), in blackface, as usual.*

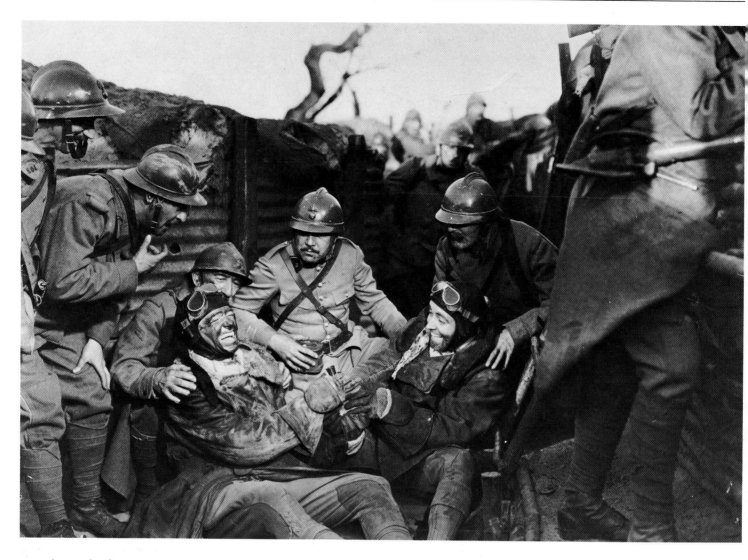

squadron of volunteer American fliers in the Royal Air Force who hate their commander (Neil Hamilton) because he must send them on missions that too often end in death. When the commander is assigned elsewhere, his place is taken by the pilot (Richard Barthelmess) who has been his most outspoken critic and who now quickly learns that death is inevitable and that commanding officers are helpless to shelter their men from it. He is then criticized by his closest friend (Douglas Fairbanks Jr). The film ends with Fairbanks taking command of the squadron and learning the terrible truth for himself.

Directed by Howard Hawks and marked with virile performances, *The Dawn Patrol* was more than exciting filmfare. It was an unusual offering because of its basic theme, a theme that Hollywood had not fully undertaken before – the loneliness and the draining responsibilities that go with command. It was a theme that war movies would use again and again in the coming years, perhaps most effectively in two post-World War II successes, *Command Decision* (1948) and *Twelve O'Clock High* (1949).

Moby Dick (1930) gave John Barrymore a second chance at playing Captain Ahab – a more impressive treatment of the story than *The Sea Beast* (1926) had been. This may well have been his finest screen performance. The love interest was supplied by Joan Bennett (Barrymore had wanted his wife Dolores Costello again, but she was pregnant).

Outward Bound (1930) told of a young man's thoughts after he and his girl friend have made an unsuccessful suicide attempt. The movie took place on a phantom ship that is going nowhere. The rest of the people on board, unbe-

knownst to the hero, are dead. The hero and heroine were played by Douglas Fairbanks and Helen Chandler, while Leslie Howard made his talking picture debut as one of the dead souls. All in all, it was a deeply moving drama.

In 1930, Warner Bros. released *Sunny* and the studio knew it had a winner. The original Broadway show with a book and lyrics by Oscar Hammerstein II and music by Jerome Kern had been a triumph for Marilyn Miller. The first musical on which Hammerstein and Kern had teamed up, it ran for 517 performances. Hammerstein later described *Sunny* as: 'One of those tailor-made affairs in which [we] . . . contrived to fit a collection of important theatrical talents. Our job was to tell a story with a cast that had been assembled as if for a revue.'

But even with all those elements, the play was essentially a vehicle for Marilyn Miller. She played Sunny Peters, a circus horseback rider in Southampton, England. A World War I US Army regiment from New York shows up, singing 'Sunny.' Tom Warren, one of the soldiers, is now returning home, and his love, Sunny, cannot accompany him unless she remarries Jim Deming, the circus owner whom she divorced a few years earlier. She won't do this and stows away aboard the ship that Tom is taking home.

Once again, Warners got the irrepressible Marilyn Miller to repeat her stage triumph in a film. Also seen were Joe Donahue, Laurence Gray, O P Heggie, Inez Courtney, Barbara Bedford, Judith Visselli and Clyde Cook. In addition to 'Sunny' and 'Who?,' the film score included 'Two Little Love Birds,' 'D'ya Love Me?' and 'I Was Alone.'

Edward G Robinson arrived from Broadway to make *The Widow from Chicago* (1930) for Warner Bros. – a picture that probably should not have been made. Robinson was a Prohibition gangster who kills a policeman. Alice White, the sister of the officer, vows to kill Robinson, and that's all.

But the following year Robinson scored in *Little Caesar* (1931), and his boast that 'No buzzard like you will ever put the cuffs on Rico' set the tone for this hard-hitting gangster movie. *Little Caesar* was the first of Warner Bros.' social

consciousness films about crime, and it was a masterpiece. It was, as so many of them were, done on the cheap, but that meant that sleazy, low-budget sets were used which only heightened the impact. Based on the life of Al Capone, it told of the rise and fall of an Italian mobster, but the surprise was Robinson, who was not what anyone would have called handsome, and who certainly had a voice to match. No

Right: *Edward G Robinson, as Rico, has a henchman get him into a speakeasy the hard way in* Little Caesar *(1931).*
Opposite: *Two World War I fighter pilots (Douglas Fairbanks Jr, left, and Richard Barthelmess) have a drink in a French trench in* The Dawn Patrol *(1930).*

Below: *Marilyn Miller and Joe Donahue share a romantic moment among the horsemen in* Sunny *(1930).*

matter, he became a star with this picture, and turned in a performance of the cold, ignorant and merciless killer driven by the desire for power that was so compelling that *The New York Times* likened the character to a figure in a Greek tragedy.

The truth was that Robinson was afraid of guns and the studio had to go so far as to tape his eyelids open every time he fired one to prevent him from blinking. The movie also made stars of Darryl F Zanuck, the production head; Hal Wallis, the producer; and Mervyn Le Roy, the director, who had been characterized by Jack Warner as 'a great director, with a small g.' Also in the cast were Douglas Fairbanks Jr and Glenda Farrell.

Warner Bros. brought the Broadway stars William Gaxton and Helen Broderick west to star in the film version of *Fifty Million Frenchmen* (1931), and the supporting stars included the comedy team of Ole Olsen and Chick Johnson. The plot was simple – basically a spoof of American tourists in France. Violet Hildegarde (Helen Broderick) was a bored American looking for shocking experiences; one of her favorite pastimes was sending risqué postcards back home. Peter Forbes (William Gaxton), a wealthy playboy, falls in love with Looloo Carroll from Terre Haute, Indiana. Forbes bets $25,000 that he can live for a month in Paris without any funds. He gets a job as a guide, becomes a gigolo and an Arabian magician, and wins both the bet and the girl. Some of the fine Cole Porter songs were retained, including 'You've Got That Thing,' 'You Do Something to Me,' 'Find Me a Primitive Man,' 'I Worship You' and 'The Tale of an Oyster.' For some reason or other, George M Cohan's 'You Remind Me of My Mother' was also added.

A pretty rotten picture that was a semi-hit anyway, owed its success to its leading lady, Barbara Stanwyck. It was *Illicit* (1931), and it told the story of a young wife whose husband (James Rennie) begins to have affairs with other women. She walks out on him, but because of the Production Code, Warners had her walk back in at the end.

The first time that Warners released *The Maltese Falcon* (1931), it starred Ricardo Cortez as Sam Spade, with Bebe Daniels as Brigid and Dudley Digges as Gutman. Actually, it was an excellent and suspenseful film, if a bit melodramatic, but it was eclipsed by the John Huston version of 1941.

The Public Enemy (1931) made a superstar out of James Cagney, who made his role as Tom Powers into a cocky, vicious thug who nevertheless, at the core, was a troubled human being with a strong sense of personal honor. Somehow audiences felt empathy for a gangster who pushes a breakfast grapefruit into the face of his girl friend, Mae Clarke. The shocked look on her face was a real one, because Cagney had promised that the grapefruit would not touch her and the whole thing would still look genuine because of a tricky camera angle.

The film told the story of Powers, a petty Chicago thief who rises to the top of the mobs during Prohibition. The plot was extremely realistic, and the movie remains a classic. But in the light of the blood baths so lovingly staged in their every gory detail in today's films, *The Public Enemy* is very interesting for its lack of visual violence. The picture is punctuated by

Below: *Ricardo Cortez, playing Sam Spade, gets a late night telephone call in the original film version of Dashiell Hammett's* The Maltese Falcon *(1931).*

Above: *James Cagney expresses his disapproval of Mae Clark's behavior by smearing her with a grapefruit – the one scene in* The Public Enemy *(1931) that no one ever forgot.*

killings, but only one – the gunning down in the street of Cagney's best friend (Edward Woods) – is actually seen by the audience. An early killing takes place in the dark and is marked only by flashes of gunfire. In another sequence, Cagney draws a gun and prepares to kill a double-crossing friend while the friend desperately tries to distract him by playing the piano; in the instant before Cagney pulls the trigger, the camera pans across the room to where Edward Woods stands watching, with the shots then being heard by the audience while the death is reflected in Woods' face.

Cagney's own end comes when, seeking revenge for Woods' murder, he slaughters a rival gang during a restaurant meeting. The camera watches him enter the restaurant and then remains out on the street while the audience listens to the rattle of gunfire inside. A moment later, the mortally wounded Cagney reappears and staggers along the street, at last collapsing in the gutter. But the picture's greatest visual violence comes in the grapefruit scene because it is so intimate. Also in the cast were Jean Harlow, Joan Blondell and Donald Cook.

Night Nurse (1931), a terrible melodrama, starred Barbara Stanwyck. She played a nurse who is assigned to a case involving a drug addict and a chauffeur and their plot to starve two young children to gain the inheritance of the children's mother. The movie's only distinction was the fact that Clark Gable played the brutal chauffeur, having replaced James Cagney, who was thought to be too important for a supporting role after the success of *The Public Enemy*.

Besides the photography which earned an Academy Award nomination, the best thing about *Svengali* (1931) was the makeup. John Barrymore chewed the scenery as Svengali, Marion Marsh's Trilby and Bramwell Fletcher's suitor were insipid. But when Barrymore mesmerized his protegé, Trilby, the makeup man blotted out his irises with cavernous white holes. The George du Maurier story, however, deserved better treatment. An English remake in 1951 with Donald Wolfit is not much better.

In a move that was later imitated by Universal Studios when they released *Frankenstein meets the Wolf Man* (1943), Warner Bros. realized that it had winners in *Little Caesar* and *The Public Enemy*, so they cast both their stars in a single picture – *Smart Money* (1931). Robinson was really the star, as a lucky barber who becomes a big-time gambler, while Cagney was one of his customers. Of course they were both given their comuppances when they ventured into illegal gambling. Boris Karloff also had a small part in the film.

The Last Flight (1931) was a lost generation movie about four wounded airmen after World War I who realize that they can't go home again. Following the Armistice they pursue wine, women and song in Paris. The film was compelling, complex and creative, and the cast was grand – Richard Barthelmess, Helen Chandler, Elliott Nugent, David Manners, Walter Byron and John Mack Brown.

James Cagney and Joan Blondell were a perfect team in *Blonde Crazy* (1931). He was a con-man bellhop and she was his chambermaid partner. Cagney, ever pugnacious, walked out on his $450 per week contract after the success of the film, and Jack Warner was forced to give him a new one for five years at $1000 per week. Featuring Louis Calhern and 26-year-old Ray Milland, the movie also had music: 'When

Your Lover Has Gone,' 'I Can't Write the Words,' 'I'm Just a Fool in Love with You' and 'Ain't That the Way It Goes?'

George Arliss returned in 1931 with another of his screen biographies. This time it was *Alexander Hamilton*. Arliss and Mary Hamplin had written it as a play years before, and he successfully repeated his Broadway role. The film was filled with period details and dealt with Hamilton's alleged affair with a married woman. Brightening up the cast were Alan Mowbray as George Washington, Charles Middleton as Justice John Jay, Montagu Love as Thomas Jefferson, Gwendolin Logan as Martha Washington and Doris Kenyon as Hamilton's wife Betsy Schuyler.

Warner Bros. resurrected an oldie for their next musical film. *Mademoiselle Modiste* had opened on Broadway in 1905, and been revived often since then. The story was a typically light operetta. Fifi works in Mme Cecile's hat shop on the Rue de la Paix. She is in love with Captain Etienne de Bouvray, but his family forbids him to marry a shopgirl. An American millionaire, Hiram Bent, becomes interested in Fifi and pays for her singing lessons. As the famous 'Mme Bellini' Fifi entertains at a charity affair at the Bouvray chateau and impresses the Comte Henri de Bouvray so much that he allows her to marry Etienne.

The Warner version of *Mademoiselle Modiste*, shot in primitive Technicolor and retitled *Kiss Me Again*, was released in 1931. Walter Pidgeon and Bernice Claire as the lovers were supported by Edward Everett Horton, Claude Gillingwater and Frank McHugh. As usual, some songs from the original score were retained. Among them 'Kiss Me Again,' 'The Mascot of the Troop,' 'The Time and the Place

and the Girl,' 'I Want What I Want When I Want It' and 'The Nightingale and the Star.'

Road to Singapore (1931), despite its title, had nothing to do with Bob Hope, Bing Crosby or Dorothy Lamour. It was the first of William Powell's nine movies at Warners. Doris Kenyon commits adultery with Powell, but is caught by her husband, Louis Calhern. The film was no winner, except in the area of most platitudes per reel.

Haunted Gold (1932) was memorable only for the fact that it was John Wayne's first appearance in a Warner Bros. film. Actually, it was a remake of a 1929 western, *The Phantom City*, which starred Ken Maynard. Wayne and Sheila Terry outwit a gang of bandits who are looking for a gold mine.

A blond Bette Davis made her first of many appearances at Warners in *The Man Who Played God* (1932), opposite George Arliss. This tear-jerker told of a concert pianist (Arliss) who is deafened by the blast of an anarchist's bomb. He is befriended by a young girl (the 24-year-old Davis) and falls in love with her. When he finds out that, although she is willing to marry him out of pity, she doesn't love him, he gives her up to another man with whom she can be happy. Arliss gave Davis her first big break when he picked her personally for the role.

With Ruth Chatterton (billed as '*Miss* Ruth Chatterton'), Bette Davis, George Brent and John Miljan, plus Orry-Kelly's beautiful gowns, how could *The Rich Are Always With Us* (1932) miss? The answer was 'easily.' Advertised as 'witty, naughty and gay . . . a spectacular story of how the other half lives – and loves – and lies,' its plot concerned Chatterton's filing for divorce from Miljan over Brent's advances, then

Right: *The frustrated Richard Barthelmess prepares to leave as the sulking Bette Davis fumes in* Cabin in the Cotton *(1932).*
Opposite: *The deaf pianist (George Arliss) looks tenderly at the young Bette Davis in* The Man Who Played God *(1932).*

Below right: *Convict James Allen (Paul Muni) being threatened by a brutal chain gang guard in* I Am a Fugitive From a Chain Gang *(1932).*

returning to her husband when he is banged up in a car accident, while Davis played a flapper flirting with Brent. The ads also called it a 'sumptuous portrayal of sensuous society in the perfumed fragrance of Park Avenue and Paris boudoirs,' but the movie was merely a trifle. The only thing to be said for it was that Brent and Chatterton fell in love during the production of the picture and married soon after.

Tiger Shark (1932) was possibly a forerunner of *Jaws* (1975), but it was far more interesting. Edward G Robinson played a Portuguese tuna fisherman with a hook for a left hand, having lost the hand in an argument with a shark. He loses his wife (Zita Johann) to his friend (Richard Arlen) and ends up being entirely consumed by a shark. It may sound corny, but the performances were stellar and the script did not sentimentalize the proceedings.

One film that deserved more praise than it received was *Life Begins* (1932), which took place in a maternity ward. Aline MacMahon was the dominating but compassionate head nurse, and almost stole the show. But Loretta Young was also fine in her role as a pregnant girl on maternal leave from prison where she has begun a sentence for murder. Frank McHugh, Gilbert Roland and Glenda Farrell also gave strong performances. Probably most people stayed away because they had learned that Young dies in childbirth in the final reel, but the scene of the heartbroken McHugh leaving the ward will never be forgotten by those who saw the film.

Cabin in the Cotton (1932) was memorable for only two reasons. First of all, it gave Bette Davis her first chance to play a bitchy Southern belle. And it also gave her a line that became one of her personal favorites: 'Ah'd love to kiss yuh,

but ah jes' washed mah hay-uh.' Otherwise, it was pretty trashy. Richard Barthelmess, in one of his last roles, was a sharecropper's son who is bewitched by Davis who, of course, merely leads him on. The picture amounted to nothing, and there was also tension on the set. Director Michael Curtiz had not wanted Davis in the film and once called her a 'Goddamned nothing, no-good sexless son of a bitch,' getting his genders confused.

One of Warners' most eloquent social protest films, *I Am a Fugitive from a Chain Gang* was also released in 1932. Paul Muni starred as James Allen, a down-on-his-luck veteran of World War I who is framed in a holdup and sentenced to work on a Georgia prison chain gang. The brutalities he experiences were enough to curdle the blood of the audiences in the theater. Allen escapes to Chicago, becomes successful in business and gets married. But he is betrayed by his wife when he returns to prison thinking that he will be paroled in three months. His parole is denied and he escapes again, knowing that he will spend the rest of his life as a hunted fugitive.

Warners' first great prison film was *20,000 Years in Sing Sing* (1933), based upon the book by Warden Lewis E Lawes of that New York state prison. Spencer Tracy played the lead – that of a man who confessed to a crime that he did not commit – and lost his life in the electric chair. The movie combined first class entertainment with a plea for prison reform. Tracy was on loan from Fox after James Cagney, during one of his frequent salary hassles with Jack Warner, turned it down. Bette Davis was her usual splendid self playing the role of Tracy's moll.

Joe E Brown finally got a part that he could do justice to in *Elmer the Great* (1933). This film version of the Ring Lardner-George M Cohan play was right down his alley. The hero was a baseball player of much talent but limited intellect, and Brown had played minor league baseball as a youth. Elmer, the home-run hitter, almost misses the big game because of his involvement with gamblers, but shows up to win the contest for the Chicago Cubs.

As far as movie musicals were concerned, the infant motion picture industry had overplayed its hand in the late 1920s. The public was fed up to the teeth with one partly or fully Technicolor song-and-dance epic after another. Grosses for musicals plunged, plans for new musicals were cancelled, and some theater owners began making it a point to advertise that their current attractions were not musicals. If the movie musical were to make a comeback, discipline was needed, and a man named Busby Berkeley emerged to provide that discipline. He did it when he directed the dance numbers in *Forty-Second Street* (1933).

Actually, the reincarnation of the musical picture might be credited to Darryl F Zanuck, the head of the production department at Warner Bros. His instincts told him that the musical was anything but dead, that nothing more was at work than the end of the musical's first cycle and that what was needed to restore the infant to favor was a solidly good film. He decided to gamble on an extravaganza. Casting his planned effort with such veterans as Warner Baxter, Bebe Daniels and George Brent, plus some talented newcomers, Zanuck went into production with *Forty-Second Street* in the latter half of 1932.

Franklin D Roosevelt had been inaugurated and told the American public that 'The only thing we have to fear is fear itself.' These magic words made 'Confidence' the slogan of the time, and Hollywood raced to do its bit to restore the public's belief in the future by reviving the corpse of the movie musical. Billed as 'A New Deal in Entertainment,' *Forty-Second Street* was just what the public wanted.

Thanks to Berkeley's direction of the musical numbers and a marvelous cast, the picture was a blockbuster. The film's plot was borrowed from an earlier Warner picture, *On With the Show* (1929), which was a story about a hatcheck girl who replaces the hard-to-handle lead in a Broadway show and wins instant stardom. In *Forty-Second Street* we see just how much work it is to mount a Broadway musical. Julian Marsh (Warner Baxter), a middle-age producer, sets out to make what he knows will be his last show. But his female lead (Bebe Daniels) breaks her leg on the night before the opening.

Marsh promotes a talented but inexperienced girl from

Above: *Bette Davis comforts the soon-to-be electrocuted Spencer Tracy in* 20,000 Years in Sing Sing *(1933).*

Opposite: *Warner Baxter giving Ruby Keeler a hard time* – Forty Second Street *(1933). Ginger Rogers is at the right.*

the chorus line (Ruby Keeler), rehearses her for a day, and with the words 'Sawyer, you're going out a youngster, but you've got to come back a star' (trite now, but dramatic then), sends her on stage. Up to that point *Forty-Second Street* didn't really look like a musical, but rather a backstage melodrama. Then Berkeley took over.

If one thing was the Busby Berkeley trademark, it was the camera shot from high above the action, showing the dancers and chorus girls moving in marvelous patterns. As he told it, the idea for that camera shot came to him one day at Warner Bros. when he climbed into the rafters to look at one of his numbers, was impressed with the view and said to himself 'I better bring the audience up here and let them see it.' To do that he literally had to cut a hole in the roof of the sound stage, but the results fascinated movie audiences and quickly set a style for the whole decade of the 1930s.

Shooting from above, Berkeley had his chorus girls go through precision routines that gave wonderful images of changing patterns, resembling the sights seen through a kaleidoscope. The straight-down camera angle was so popular that it was quickly imitated by many directors who didn't have Berkeley's imagination, so it soon became a laughable cliché. But in its early days, the new camera angle was a real eye-opener.

It wasn't just the 'top shot' that made Busby Berkeley musicals so spectacular – it was a zany kind of imagination that used the camera as few directors had dared to use it before. In *Forty-Second Street* Berkeley started the big number by showing Ruby Keeler doing a solo dance. As the camera pulled back, the audience saw that she was dancing on top of a taxicab, and that the taxi was parked in the middle of 42nd Street in Manhattan. Until that point, the number is supposed to be part of a Broadway musical, but no theater stage could hold the spectacular mass of scenery and dancers that Busby Berkeley used.

The production numbers in *Forty-Second Street* were superb. The audience was treated to the 'Shuffle Off to Buffalo' number featuring a newlywed couple (Keeler and Clarence Nordstrom) eager to spend their first night together aboard a Niagara Falls-bound train, only to have their Pullman car keep them apart by dividing itself into many berths, all filled with chorus girls who have a thoroughly good time making cynical fun of the honeymooners.

Then there was the 'Young and Healthy' sequence, which began with Dick Powell singing and evolved into a team of chorus girls and boys dancing on a revolving stage and forming that old Berkeley trademark – patterns photographed from overhead.

Then came the previously mentioned finale – the number from which the picture took its title. Intended to portray New York's fast-paced and decadent night life, the sequence began with an evening-gowned Keeler singing 'Forty-Second Street,' after which she drops her long skirt for a tap dance atop the taxicab. To the song's pulsating rhythms, the camera moved up the crowded street, encountered various Broadway types along the way, witnessed an attack on a girl and then a stabbing, staying with these occurrences only an instant as it fell in with columns of chorus girls tap dancing along the street. At last, male dancers joined the girls and together, with painted boards, they formed a rising and almost surreal skyline of New York. The number closed with Keeler and Powell looming above the skyline and waving to the audience.

The superbly choreographed sequences dazzled audiences and established Berkeley as the premier dance director of the period. But it would be unfair to say that *Forty-Second Street*'s appeal lay in his efforts alone. Even without its extravagant ending, the picture would have had an attraction to audiences of the 1930s. It told a harsh story of struggle and hard work. It told it with bitter wisecracks and with Baxter's excellent aura of exhaustion and disillusionment – his role was one of the outstanding characterizations of his career. It played the story against a tawdry backdrop of chorines' apartments and sweaty rehearsal halls. And, in the midst of the exultation at its close, it sounded a grim note – a hard-

faced Baxter looking at the stage and knowing that his life's work is over. In all, the film dealt with tough realities that Depression-era audiences understood and that aroused a definite emotional response in them, and director Lloyd Bacon should be given much of the credit for this. When these realities were blended with Berkeley's escapist production numbers, *Forty-Second Street* became a perfectly but eerily balanced Depression product.

This was the classic 'putting on a show' musical that started Hollywood's golden age of musicals, combining genuine backstage atmosphere with a caustic script, and a marvelous cast. Admittedly, Ruby Keeler had to make a small talent go a long way – but she succeeded. Aside from Baxter and Keeler, the movie had George Brent and Bebe Daniels, both veterans; Dick Powell, who had sung with a band; and an up-and-coming sexy starlet with a peppery personality, appropriately named Ginger. Ms Rogers was destined to become one of the hottest musical stars ever.

The critics went wild. *The New York Times* called it 'The liveliest and one of the most tuneful screen musical comedies that has come out of Hollywood.'

For some reason, Warner Bros. thought that they had to have a live stage show to accompany the opening of *Forty-Second Street* at the Strand Theater in New York City. But none of the stars of the picture was in it. The ads read 'AND . . . IN PERSON brought to you direct from Hollywood on the famous "42nd Street" Special – Joe E Brown, Tom Mix, Bette Davis, Laura La Plante, Glenda Farrell, Lyle Talbot, Leo Carillo, Claire Dodd, Preston Foster, Eleanor Holm.'

William Berkeley Enos, alias Busby Berkeley, was now established in Hollywood. He struck back as the musical director of *Gold Diggers of 1933* (1933), in which he showed girls in a peep-show silhouette scene in a way that suggested nudity. Berkeley seemed to have a license to titillate, and used the stage tradition of the undressed chorus girl to get away with every breach of Will Hays' Production Code possible and still get the seal of approval.

Gold Diggers of 1933 was loosely based on the Avery Hopwood Broadway play about a group of girls in search of millionaire husbands. Warners' had made a silent version in 1923. In this film, Berkeley had a number that started with the camera zooming in on a singer whose profile turns into a city skyline. Free-flowing geometric designs formed by neon-lit violins filled the screen during 'The Shadow Waltz.' The one serious note was Joan Blondell's singing 'Remember My Forgotten Man' to a chorus of the unemployed – a reminder that many of the soldiers and sailors who fought in World War I were lucky if they could sell apples in the street during the Great Depression-plagued year of 1933.

Ginger Rogers was back in this film, playing a conniving little thing eager to make it big. Her name in the film was Fay Fortune, proving that Warner Bros. figured that subtlety was a waste of time. Joan Blondell and Aline MacMahon provided sparkle and humor to the movie.

Blondell and Dick Powell appeared together for the first time in the picture, but they were to go on together and set a record for the number of times a team co-starred in musical films – ten. This record was later tied by Fred Astaire and Ginger Rogers. Also, little did anyone know that Powell, the crooning juvenile, would later emerge as a tough but likeable leading man in serious non-musicals, a competent director and an ambitious producer – the founder of Four Star Television.

Footlight Parade (1933), another in the Powell-Keeler-

Blondell mold, was important because it gave James Cagney his first singing and dancing role in the movies. Cagney had started his stage career as a song-and-dance man. In the early 1920s, when he was struggling to support his family with the occasional song-and-dance engagement, he got a big break – he landed a job with an up-and-coming vaudeville group. The performer he replaced was a young Englishman named Archibald Leach, who later would gain renown as Cary Grant. In one number in *Footlight Parade*, Cagney wore a sailor suit as he danced on a tabletop with Keeler (dressed in a Chinese costume) – an omen of the scores of Navy musicals that were to come.

Again, Berkeley made fireworks with tiers and towers of girls who looked like they were made of spun sugar. For the

Opposite: *One of the glorious Busby Berkeley routines. This is the 'By a Waterfall' number in* Footlight Parade *(1933).*

Above: *Ruby Keeler and Dick Powell. The two stars of* Gold Diggers of 1933 *(1933) – her second and his fifth film.*

'By a Waterfall' number, he built an aquacade that use hydraulic lifts to move 100 chorus girls and had 20,000 gallons of water per minute pumped as the girls tumbled down into a studio-built lake. This scene was a forerunner of Esther Williams' bathing beauty musicals for MGM in the 1940s and 50s. Indeed, it was Berkeley who choreographed Williams' biggest hit, *Million Dollar Mermaid* (1952).

In *Lady Killer* (1933), James Cagney didn't push a grapefruit in Mae Clarke's face – he just pulled her out of bed by her hair. Cagney played the part of an usher in a movie theater who turns to crime after he loses his job. While he is on the lam, somehow he ends up appearing in a film and becomes a star. Pretty silly, but Cagney's vitality and self-confidence saved the day and made the movie a sparkling comedy.

Right: *Berkeley outdid himself in the number 'The Shadow Waltz,' from* Gold Diggers of 1933 *(1933), where chorus girls formed geometric designs with their neon-lit violins.*

Below: *Another view of the violin-playing chorines in 'The Shadow Waltz' from* Gold Diggers of 1933. *This is one of Busby Berkeley's patented shoot-from-the-ceiling scenes.*

Pat O'Brien had a role that presaged his appearance as Knute Rockne in *College Coach* (1933). Supposed to be a satire, the film went off on a tangent near the end, but O'Brien as the aggressive coach was quite good, as were Arthur Byron as the college president and Ann Dvorak as O'Brien's wife. Poor Dick Powell was given the role of a football player because of his box office power, but he was pathetic – his tough guy roles were not to come for a decade.

Lionel Atwill played the mentally and physically scarred proprietor of a wax museum in *The Mystery of the Wax Museum* (1933), one of Warners' rare ventures into the world of the horror film. But it was a stunner, especially at the end when the museum catches fire and the wax figures grotesquely melt down and when the terrified Fay Wray scratches at Atwill's face, crumbling his wax mask to reveal

his horrible appearance. Glenda Farrell and Frank McHugh also starred in the movie, which was shot in Technicolor.

Fashions of 1934 (1934) starred William Powell and Bette Davis. It was a trivial but enjoyable romp about con-man Powell and designer Davis conquering the Paris fashion world. The show-stopper was 'The Hall of Human Harps' production number in which it appeared that the chorus girls were part of the structure of dozens of harps. One critic said, 'The theme song of mothers of stage-struck daughters might well be "I didn't raise my daughter to be a human harp."'

The first outing of co-stars Barbara Stanwyck and Joel McCrea revealed a great chemistry between them – something that Warners would later exploit. The film was *Gambling Lady* (1934), in which Stanwyck played the

Right: *Band singer Tommy (Dick Powell) and cabaret dancer Inez (Dolores Del Rio) share a tender moment in* Wonder Bar *(1934).*

Below: *Lionel Atwill contemplates a wax mask in* The Mystery of the Wax Museum *(1933).*

daughter of a gambler who had committed suicide when he couldn't pay off his debts. She decides to carry on the family tradition and goes to the gambling tables where she meets McCrea. After some complications of murder, blackmail and robbery, all ends well. Also in the cast were Pat O'Brien, C Aubrey Smith and Arthur Treacher.

When Warner Bros. released the film version of *Wonder Bar* in 1934, it was a fascinating melange. Al Jolson played the part of Al Wonder, owner of a Paris night club. He and his band singer, Tommy (Dick Powell), are both in love with the cabaret star, Ynez (Dolores Del Rio), but she is only interested in her dance partner, Harry (Ricardo Cortez). Her rival for Harry's affection is a wealthy society girl, Laina (Kay Francis). There were also complicated subplots. Simpson (Guy Kibbee) and Pratt (Hugh Herbert), who are married to Louise Fazenda and Ruth Donnelly, respectively, are chasing two of the club's hostesses, Mitzi (Fifi D'Orsay) and Claire (Merna Kennedy, who was married at the time to Busby

Berkeley, the musical director of the film). A German officer, Captain von Ferring (Robert Barrat), spends his last night at the Wonder Bar before killing himself. Del Rio stabs Cortez when she learns he is leaving her for Francis. Del Rio then falls for Powell and Jolson steps aside.

This was not Berkeley's best work, but one number, 'Don't Say Goodnight,' was vintage Berkeley. First sung by Powell, it was then danced by Cortez and Del Rio, before turning into a fantasy in the classic Berkeley manner. Other songs in the movie were 'Why Do I Dream These Dreams?,' 'Vive La France,' 'Tango Del Rio' and 'Wonder Bar.'

Another Dick Powell-Ruby Keeler-Joan Blondell film with a plot similar to those that had gone before, *Dames*, was released in 1934. The movie was another paean to Berkeley's imaginative talent. In the 'I Only Have Eyes for You' number, he had Keeler's image multiplied endlessly when chorus girls donned masks of her face. Another incredible number was 'When You Were a Smile on Your Mother's Lips and a Twinkle in Your Daddy's Eye.'

On a more serious plane, *The Key* (1934) was a story about the Black and Tans in Ireland during the Troubles. William Powell was a British Army captain who claimed that he had been decorated three times – once for bravery, twice for indiscretions. He proceeds to have an affair with Edna Best, the wife of a British Intelligence officer, Colin Clive. But he redeems himself with an act of bravery.

One of the early Perry Mason films starred Warren William, who had also played Philo Vance. It was *The Case of the Howling Dog* (1934), and it kept the audience wondering until the end whether co-star Mary Astor was guilty or not. It was unique for the time in that it used no background music except for one point when a radio is turned on and blares out the title tune from *Dames*.

Gold Diggers of 1935 (1935) gave Berkeley a chance to direct an entire movie, not just the musical parts. Still he did not stint when it came to the songs, most of which resembled a three-ring circus. In what many critics regard as the finest example of his work – 'The Lullaby of Broadway' sequence, sung by Wini Shaw – he traced a day and a night in the life of a chorus girl, starting quietly with her face a mere speck on the screen, and then, on expanding to full screen, whirling her through a full series of experiences that, with the background music ranging from romantic to sinister, culminates with her accidental death plunge from a balcony as Manhattan's mad and tawdry night life closes chokingly about her. An outgrowth of the 'Forty-second Street' number, it had far greater impact.

In another number, Berkeley had stagehands, who were

One of Busby Berkeley's chorus numbers 'I Only Have Eyes For You' from Dames *(1934).*

invisible because they were dressed in black, wheel 100 white pianos and their chorine players through a variety of patterns for the 'The Words Are in My Heart' production number. Actually, it appeared that the pianos were dancing while the girls sat still. All of this was expensive, an estimated $10,000 for every minute of film. But it paid off at the box office.

Devil Dogs of the Air (1935) starred James Cagney and Pat O'Brien in a salute to the flying Marines. Along the way the two of them vied for the affections of Margaret Lindsay. The story wasn't much, but the chemistry between Cagney and O'Brien was something to watch, and the special effects were authentic. The film was lauded for giving an accurate view of Marine air training and is remembered today chiefly for its top-notch aerial stunt sequences.

Warners' crime movies changed a bit in 1935 as a result of the 1933 ruling by the Production Code Authority that gangsterism should not be glorified and the Catholic Legion of Decency also made the same demand. So James Cagney went over to the good guys side in *G-Men* (1935). He was a lawyer (a requirement of the Federal Bureau of Investigation at the time) who joined the Feds to avenge the murder of a friend. The film was action-packed and ran at rollercoaster velocity. Cagney had not been this good since *The Public Enemy*. Also in the cast were Margaret Lindsay, Ann Dvorak, Barton MacLane and Robert Armstrong.

The Traveling Saleslady (1935) starred Joan Blondell

(finally getting top billing), Glenda Farrell, William Gargan and Hugh Herbert. It was a rollicking comedy with Blondell being a woman who sells 'The Cocktail Toothpaste' – whiskey flavor in the morning, martini flavoring in the afternoon and champagne flavor before bed.

Warren William was back as Perry Mason in *The Case of the Curious Bride* (1935). He helps Margaret Lindsay out when he finds out that her husband, who was supposed to be dead, was indeed alive. The only thing to recommend the picture was that Errol Flynn made his film debut as a corpse in it.

The old baseball player, Joe E Brown, made another diamond film, and it was his best of the genre – *Alibi Ike* (1935). It told the story of an eccentric baseball player to whom everything that can happen, does. Miscast in the film as the love interest was Olivia de Havilland, but the story was by Ring Lardner, and that's all that mattered.

Al Jolson's magnetic personality ramrodded its way through Warners' *Go Into Your Dance* (1935). He co-starred with his then wife, Ruby Keeler, in this backstage musical about an arrogant Broadway star who is so unlovable that he finds he can't get a job. Of course Keeler, as a cute little night club dancer, reforms him and helps him to open a New York casino. He has a little trouble with the mob, but since this was a musical and not one of Warners' crime specials, everything worked itself out. The music was excellent, and two of the production numbers have become classics – 'About a

Quarter to Nine' and 'A Latin from Manhattan.' Other songs were 'The Little Things You Used to Do,' 'Cielito Lindo,' 'Go Into Your Dance,' 'Mammy,' 'I'll Sing About You,' 'A Good Old-Fashioned Cocktail with a Good Old-Fashioned Girl' and 'Casino De Paree.' Also in the cast were Helen Morgan, Glenda Farrell, Barton MacLane and Patsy Kelly.

Few people could understand why Warners tried to make William Shakespeare's *A Midsummer Night's Dream* (1935), but make it they did, although they must have known that it would not be popular with the Depression-era audiences. It has been called 'the studio's burnt offering to culture in general and Shakespeare in particular.' Max Reinhardt, the great European stage director, was hired to do the job, but it became evident that he was not used to movie making, and one of his former students, the successful film director William Dieterle, was called in to assist. A ton of money was spent on the forest scenes, where fake trees had real leaves glued on them, which were then painted silver. The photography was exceptional, and the special effects were wonderful, especially in the fairy sequences.

But James Cagney as Bottom, Olivia de Havilland as Hermia and Dick Powell as Lysander were terrible. Mickey Rooney was a fine Puck, but he broke his leg halfway through production and had to be wheeled around on a bicycle which was cleverly hidden behind the bushes. Along with Rooney, Victor Jory as Oberon and Anita Louise as Titania were more than acceptable. The best performance of all, however, came from none other than Joe E Brown as Flute. This production was a great blow to both Shakespeare and box office receipts from which American films have never recovered.

Pat O'Brien and James Cagney were at it again in *The Irish in Us* (1935). Frank McHugh joined them and they played three tough brothers who were nonetheless bossed around by their Irish mother, Mary Gordon (every time Warners needed a pleasant, yet stern mother with a brogue so thick that a leprechaun would have trouble understanding it, they called on Mary Gordon). Cagney was the cocky, out of work brother who became a fight manager, but had to enter the ring himself when his fighter turned up drunk. He won the girl (Olivia de Havilland) and the fight. Others in the cast from the Warner Bros. Stock Company were Allen Jenkins and J Farrell MacDonald.

Up to the time when Jack Warner cast him as the hero of *Captain Blood* (1935), Errol Flynn had been seen on screen in only two movies for a total of about seven minutes. Of course Jack had wanted Robert Donat for the role, but had to settle for Flynn – a most fortuitous happenstance. Flynn played Peter Blood, an English surgeon, sentenced to slavery for his part in Monmouth's Rebellion. He escapes and becomes a pirate. No swashes were left unbuckled, and Flynn's duel with Basil Rathbone as a rival French pirate was a masterpiece. The film made stars of Flynn and the female lead Olivia de Havilland, and they were to co-star in a total of seven films together.

The Story of Louis Pasteur (1936) rekindled Warner Bros.'

Right: *Humphrey Bogart, playing Duke Mantee, confronts the itinerant poet (Leslie Howard) and the would-be artist (Bette Davis) in* The Petrified Forest *(1936).*
Opposite top: *Errol Flynn, playing the title role in* Captain Blood *(1935) leads his men in taking over a ship.*

Opposite bottom: *Some of the peasants from* A Midsummer Night's Dream *(1935). Joe E Brown (second from left), as Flute, the bellows maker, stole the picture. Behind him are James Cagney as Bottom, Frank McHugh as Quince (fifth from left), Hugh Herbert (sixth from left) and Arthur Treacher (eight from left).*

faith in biographical pictures – something they had lost since the days of George Arliss. At first Jack Warner was sure that the movie would be a bomb, and allowed a mere $330,000 for its production costs – pretty small for a costume film. So the producer had to steal scenery from wherever he could – the French Academy of Science Amphitheater was left over from a Busby Berkeley night club number, for example. But Muni was magnificent as the French biochemist who found the cures for anthrax and rabies. It was a dignified triumph all the way round.

Humphrey Bogart had been in Hollywood for a while, taking on indifferent roles in indifferent films, but his big break came in *The Petrified Forest* (1936) based on the play by Robert E Sherwood. He played Duke Mantee, referred to as 'the last great apostle of rugged individualism,' but who was really an escaped killer. Bogart had played the role on Broadway, and Leslie Howard, also from the New York production, appeared as Alan Squier, one of those rarest of birds in America, an itinerant poet. Squier meets and falls in love with Bette Davis, who is a waitress working in an Arizona desert cafe and gas station but wants to be an art student in Paris. Then in comes Duke Mantee. Improbable as the story line sounds, it worked, and the result was a thundering thriller. The honesty of the film was saved by Leslie Howard. The studio wanted a happy ending of sorts, which would have killed the impact of the movie. But Howard insisted that it end as the stage play had, with Squier dying, and that was that.

Anthony Adverse was a long-awaited film. Hervey Allen's heavy tome had been almost as popular in America as *Gone With the Wind* was to be, and the audiences lined up in droves to get into the theaters. What greeted them, however, was a two hour and 16 minute endurance test. The plot was about the adventures of a young man, Anthony Adverse

(Fredric March), in nineteenth century America and Mexico. Despite the tedium, the picture was a box office smash and added to Warners' already strong costume epic prestige. Also in the cast of this historical semi-swashbuckler were Olivia de Havilland, Edmund Gwenn, Claude Rains, Anita Louise, Louis Hayward, Donald Wood, Gale Sondergaard, Akim Tamiroff and Ralph Morgan.

Bette Davis played an alcoholic actress on a run of bad luck in *Dangerous* (1936), a prolonged melodramatic cliché, although Davis won her first Academy Award for it. She had fought Warner Bros. and finally convinced them that she should look as unglamorous as possible during the first part of the film, before she is rehabilitated by a young architect (Franchot Tone). This paid off, and the movie picked up a little credibility for it.

Kay Francis played the famous nurse, Florence Nightingale, in *White Angel* (1936), and Nightingale lost. The film was filled with historical inaccuracies and Francis was woefully miscast, since her acting abilities were never more than serviceable. But the scenes at Scutari Hospital in the Crimea, with their panoramas that would be outdone only in *Gone With the Wind*, had so much impact that they almost saved the picture.

The Green Pastures (1936) was a breakthrough for its time although today it could be criticized as racist with its description of blacks as shuffling, simple-minded innocents. Warner Bros. really broke new ground in this adaptation of Marc Connelly's charming play based on the stories of Roark Bradford, describing the Bible story as it might be understood by black children in a rural Southern Sunday School. Rex Ingram was dignified and impressive as 'De Lawd,' the Hall Johnson Choir gave the film some wonderful music and Eddie 'Rochester' Anderson was outstanding as Gabriel. The picture was, however, a box office flop.

Gold Diggers of 1937 (1936) revealed a tame Busby Berkeley, a man with budget problems, although Dick Powell and Joan Blondell were their usual peppy selves, and there was a great production number, 'With Plenty of Money and You.' After 30 or so musicals at Warner Bros., Berkeley left the studio for MGM in 1938.

As David Niven later reminisced, director Michael Curtiz knew how to mangle the English language – he once shouted at a group of extras to 'Stop standing in bunches.' And during the making of *The Charge of the Light Brigade* (1936), when he wanted some riderless steeds to appear, he screamed 'Bring on the empty horses.' But he had no peer when he was directing such action-packed films as this adaptation of the Tennyson poem. The attention to detail was amazing. Actual postage stamps of the period were used, whether they could be seen by the audience or not. The uniforms were authentic – exactly like those worn by the 27th Dragoons. Of course an extended prologue set in India of the 1850s, and a fake love triangle was contrived for Errol Flynn, Olivia de Havilland and Patric Knowles, who played Flynn's brother, but only hard-core historians objected. This $1,200,000 epic was worth every penny and the charge sequences in the Crimea were breathtaking.

Another hard-hitting Warner Bros. film of social importance was *Black Legion* (1937), which starred Humphrey Bogart as a factory worker who joins the Ku Klux Klan when he is fired from his job and a foreigner is appointed in his place. Bogart finds out too late how evil and corrupt the Klan is. At the end, the courtroom judge, just before passing sentence on the corrupt Legionnaires, points out in an impassioned speech that bigotry, mob violence and terrorism are 100 percent unAmerican.

The Prince and the Pauper (1937) was based on Mark Twain's novel and was basically a picture for the young. Billy and Bobby Mauch, real twins, played the title roles and completely stole the show from Errol Flynn, who appeared as the roguish swashbuckler who helps the two boys to change identities. The final coronation scene was suitably opulent, and nicely timed, since when the picture was released Britain was celebrating the coronation of King George VI. Also in this sixteenth-century period piece were Claude Rains as the Earl of Hertford, a properly villainous portrayal, and Alan Hale as the Captain of the Guard, whose accent would not have fooled a deaf person.

Warners' best boxing film was *Kid Galahad* (1937), which today is seen on late night television as *The Battling Bellhop*, so as not to be confused with an Elvis Presley movie of 1962 called *Kid Galahad*. Edward G Robinson was great as an argumentative fight manager who finds a bellhop (Wayne Morris) who can fight. Bette Davis was Robinson's girl friend, but didn't have much of a part. Humphrey Bogart, as a crooked promoter, gave Robinson a run for the acting honors.

The Life of Emile Zola (1937) was superb. Paul Muni gave a towering performance as the French writer and social activist. It centered on the famous 'J'accuse' paper written by Zola on behalf of the disgraced Major Dreyfus, who was cashiered from the French Army and sent to Devil's Island, and whom Zola defended by saying that Dreyfus was railroaded because he was Jewish. An amazing sidelight is that in the lengthy courtroom sequence, never once is the word 'Jew' uttered.

They Won't Forget (1937) was inspired by both the real-life Leo M Frank case in 1931 and Ward Green's novel, *Death in the Deep South*. The movie told the story of a teacher who is convicted of raping and killing one of his students, a 15-year-old girl, and whose death sentence is commuted. When the teacher is released, he is lynched by the citizens of his own town. Claude Rains was memorable as the ambitious prosecuting attorney who uses the case to win himself the governor's chair in a bigoted and prejudiced Southern state. The performances were intense, including, in addition to Rains, Gloria Dickson, Otto Kruger, Allyn Joslyn, Elisha Cook and

two stars sparkled in this entertaining, funny and satiric movie. Also in the cast were Anita Louise, Basil Rathbone, Melville Cooper and Morris Carnovsky.

There is no doubt that Errol Flynn's most popular film was *The Adventures of Robin Hood* (1938). At least it is the one on which his reputation for swashbuckling and athleticism rests. And once again his finest hour was a duel with Basil Rathbone. Originally, Robin was to have been played by James Cagney with Guy Kibbee as Friar Tuck. But Jack Warner was feuding with Cagney again and changed his mind about the casting. Then he saw *Captain Blood* and knew that Flynn was the man for him (something that many young women also decided). Jack budgeted the picture at a whopping $1,600,000, which was the largest upfront money ever ticketed for a Warner picture up to that time (the movie came in at $2,000,000). About the only message in the motion picture was that good triumphs over evil, but there was enough excitement in it to equip six or seven adventure yarns. The cast included Rathbone as Sir Guy of Gisbourne, Claude Rains as Prince John, Olivia de Havilland as Maid

Above: *Paul Muni played the great French writer and humanitarian in* The Life of Emile Zola *(1937). With him is Gloria Holden.*

Above right: *Henry Fonda and Bette Davis in* Jezebel *(1938). Fonda is in a jealous mood and Davis is winning her second Oscar.*

Opposite: *Errol Flynn as the leader of the Merry Men in* The Adventures of Robin Hood *(1938). Flynn was fair with a sword, but not as good with a*

bow and arrow, so professional archer Howard Hill did his shooting for him. Other stuntwork involved dropping from trees.

Clinton Rosmand as the black janitor who finds the girl's body. The film also contained the debut of 15-year-old Lana Turner, who played the murdered girl. Her famous 'sweater scene' marked her for stardom, and she was signed by MGM the following year.

Bette Davis and Leslie Howard emerged as comedians in *It's Love I'm After* (1937), a wonderful comedy about an acting team whose marriage has been postponed 11 times. Their relationship is established in the first scene where, in a performance of *Romeo and Juliet*, they whisper ugly nothings to each other while onstage. But when Olivia de Havilland enters the picture and falls in love with Howard, Davis decides that she had better marry him herself. It was a madcap comedy which was loved both by audiences and critics.

Another rather unusual comedy team appeared in *Tovarich* (1937) – Claudette Colbert and Charles Boyer. They played a couple of aristocratic Russian emigrés down on their luck in Paris. So Colbert becomes a maid and Boyer a butler in the same house. The fun starts when they are recognized by some haughty friends of their employer. The

Marion, Patric Knowles as Will Scarlet, Eugene Pallette as Friar Tuck, Alan Hale as Little John, Melville Cooper as the Sheriff of Nottingham and Ian Hunter as King Richard the Lionhearted.

The ads for *Jezebel* (1938) called Bette Davis 'half-angel, half-siren, all woman!' The role was a pay-off from Jack Warner, who had refused to loan Davis to David O Selznick for *Gone With the Wind*. But Davis showed that she could have played Scarlett O'Hara by pouring all her talents into the role of Julia Marston, a Southern Belle who does everything she can to make her fiancé (Henry Fonda) jealous, yet goes to his bedside when he comes down with the plague. The story was based on a flop play by Owen Davis and could have been a flop movie, too, except for the presence of these two pros (Davis won an Oscar for best actress). Helping in the proceedings were Fay Bainter (who also won an Oscar for best supporting actress), George Brent and Margaret Lindsay.

Edward G Robinson rather stubbed his toe in *The Amazing Dr Clitterhouse*. He played the title role, originated on the stage by Sir Cedric Hardwicke, of a psychiatrist studying the criminal mentality who decides to become a criminal

himself in order to find out more about his subject, eventually committing a murder. Robinson came close to recapitulating his role in *Little Caesar*, and so audiences were not surprised when he switched from good guy to bad guy, but the John Wexley-John Huston screenplay was excellent, as was the direction of Anatole Litvak, and Robinson was helped along by Humphrey Bogart, Claire Trevor, Donald Crisp, John Litel and Henry O'Neill.

James Cagney and Pat O'Brien were at it again in *Angels with Dirty Faces* (1938). Cagney was Rocky Sullivan, a criminal who finds that he has become a hero in his old slum neighborhood, as far as the Dead End Kids (Billy Halop, Bobby Jordan, Leo Gorcey, Gabriel Dell, Huntz Hall, etc) are concerned. O'Brien was the local parish priest, who is disturbed about the way the boys admire a criminal. Cagney and O'Brien both came from that East Side gutter and they are friends still, but they are friends at war and one of them must be destroyed. Father Connolly admits to Sullivan that crime appears to pay. He concedes that recklessness and a distorted kind of heroism tend to glorify the gangster, to make him a juvenile idol. At the end, when Cagney is to go to the electric chair, O'Brien prevails upon him to show his courage by acting the coward in order to destroy the boys' hero-worship. Also in the fine cast were Humphrey Bogart and Ann Sheridan.

Above: *Father Connolly (Pat O'Brien) congratulates Rocky Sullivan (James Cagney), who has decided to play the coward in* Angels with Dirty Faces *(1938).*
Opposite bottom: *Basil Rathbone (left) and Errol Flynn –* Dawn Patrol *(1938).*

Brother Rat (1938) was just plain fun, and told of three cadets at a military academy and the three girls who were their one and only sweethearts. Starring were Ronald Reagan, Wayne Morris and Eddie Albert, with Priscilla Lane, Jane Wyman and Jane Bryan. The only conflict in the film was that Albert and Bryan were secretly married (against the rules of the institute), and she was pregnant.

Four Daughters (1938) was a weeper whose only claim to fame was the performance of the young John Garfield, as Mickey Borden. It told of the romances of four young girls (Rosemary Lane, Lola Lane, Priscilla Lane and Gale Page), members of a small-town American family. It was pulp fiction, but it made the performance of Garfield stand out. He played the shabby, indolent, acerbic Borden to the hilt, and he became a star.

With a somewhat abbreviated title, Warner Bros. remade *The Dawn Patrol* (1930) as *Dawn Patrol* in 1938 as an Errol Flynn-David Niven vehicle. The remake suffered by comparison because it glamorized the two leading characters, though Basil Rathbone was excellent in bringing tension to the role as the original squadron commander. Footage from the original production was used for some of the aerial sequences.

The Oklahoma Kid (1939) was a most unusual film. James Cagney played a cowboy and the role called for him to sing 'Rockabye Baby' in Spanish and 'I Don't Want to Play in Your Yard.' Humphrey Bogart was a blacker-than-black villain. Eventually Cagney takes the law into his own hands and kills Bogart. Also in the cast were Priscilla Lane, Donald Crisp, Joe Devlin, Ward Bond, John Miljan and Arthur Aylesworth.

Confessions of a Nazi Spy (1939) caused a sensation. Based on the memoirs of former Federal Bureau of Investigation agent Leon G Torrou, and very much done in a documentary style, the picture attracted probably as many policemen and special agents to its premiere as it did ticket-buying customers. This was the first American picture to deal with the Nazi espionage infiltration as a reality and to warn the world about the evil of the Nazis. Edward G Robinson led the team of G-Men who uncover the network of Nazi spies. Following the opening Robinson, Jack Warner and many others actually received threatening letters. The film, also featuring Francis Lederer, George Sanders and Paul Lukas, was banned in many countries in Europe.

Dark Victory (1939) was a smash hit both for Warner Bros. and for Bette Davis. At the beginning, Jack Warner was dubious. 'Who wants to see a dame go blind?' he said. But this four-handkerchief movie established Davis as the biggest star at the studio. Judith Traherne (Davis) is a flighty heiress who, unbeknownst to her, is suffering from a brain tumor. Davis

gave a controlled performance, especially in the scene toward the end, when she and her friend Ann (Geraldine Fitzgerald in her first American film) are planting hyacinth bulbs as she goes blind. Davis was also controlled in her heart-breaking final death scene. Other convincing performances were turned in by George Brent as the doctor she falls in love with, Humphrey Bogart, Ronald Reagan, Henry Travers and Cora Witherspoon.

Dodge City (1939) was the story of a town in Kansas in the early days, when railroads were heading west. Colonel Dodge of Dodge City summed up the railroad as 'a symbol of

Below: *Edward G Robinson, as the head G-Man, puts the cuffs on Joe Sawyer in* Confessions of a Nazi Spy *(1939).*

America's progress – iron horses and iron men.' He added, 'The West stands for honesty, courage and morality.' In the film, Errol Flynn was the embodiment of these qualities, and it is his job to clean up the town. Flanked by Guinn 'Big Boy' Williams and Alan Hale, he confronted the crooked machinations of Bruce Cabot and Victor Jory. Flynn played a wagonmaster, and his barroom brawl in the picture was a masterpiece. Along with taming the town, Flynn also tamed Olivia de Havilland. Also in the cast were Ann Sheridan, Frank McHugh, John Litel, Ward Bond and Cora Witherspoon.

Juarez (1939) was a masterpiece. Based on real events, of course, it had three interlocking subplots: the desire of Napoleon III of France to subjugate Mexico, the sad marriage of Emperor Maximilian (appointed ruler of Mexico by Napoleon) and his wife, Carlotta, and the revolution led by Benito Juarez to liberate his country and turn it into a democracy. The cast was exceptional. Paul Muni was Juarez, Claude Rains was Napoleon, Bette Davis was Carlotta, Brian Aherne was Maximilian. And the cast also included Gale Sondergaard, Donald Crisp, Joseph Calleia, Gilbert Roland and 1186 others. Only John Garfield was disappointing, but he played General Porfirio Diaz, and his accent was against him.

The explosive combination of James Cagney and George Raft was used to its fullest in *Each Dawn I Die* (1939). Cagney played a newspaper reporter who was railroaded to prison,

Below: *Errol Flynn, at the foot of the stairs, challenges a villain in Dodge City (1939). Behind him are Frank McHugh and Alan Hale.*
Right: *Paul Muni in another of his biopics – this time as Benito Juarez in* Juarez *(1939). It told the story of revolution in Mexico.*

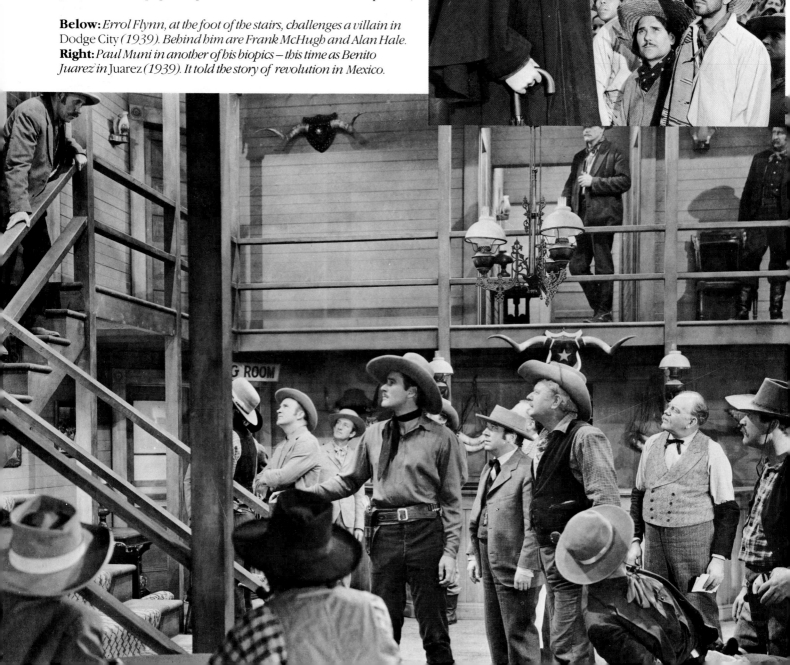

Above: *Bette Davis (right) as* The Old Maid *(1939). With her is Miriam Hopkins as the cousin who agrees to raise her daughter.*

where he meets Raft and learns about being a criminal. Also in the cast were Jane Bryan, George Bancroft, Maxie Rosenbloom and Victor Jory.

Bette Davis scored again in 1939 with *The Old Maid*, in which the 31-year-old Davis began as a young girl and aged right before the audiences eyes to a 60-year-old tight-lipped old maid. In the meantime, she has allowed her illegitimate daughter to be raised by her cousin (Miriam Hopkins) who

has married the man Davis loved. The cast included George Brent, Donald Crisp, William Lundigan and, in her last screen appearance, Louise Fazenda.

Humphrey Bogart took his turn at being a mad scientist in *The Return of Dr X* (1939). The return in this case referred to a return from the grave. Bogart was an executed child murderer, Dr Maurice Xavier, who has been brought back to life, but needed frequent transfusions of human blood to stay that way. The only decent thing about the movie was Bogart's makeup with its waxy features and white-streaked hair.

The Private Lives of Elizabeth and Essex (1939) was made

Below: *Vera Zorina, as the ballerina, comforts Eddie Albert in* On Your Toes *(1939).*

for Bette Davis, who had wanted Laurence Olivier to play the part of Essex. But the role was given to Errol Flynn, whom she thought was too inexperienced to deal with the blank verse that was taken from Maxwell Anderson's play, *Elizabeth the Queen*. Flynn seemed to agree, acting embarrassed – having a lot of bravado without a great deal of conviction in his interpretation. Director Michael Curtiz let Davis have her way with her emoting, but because of that, no one else in the cast (besides Flynn, there were Olivia de Havilland, Donald Crisp, Alan Hale and Henry Daniell) had a chance to do much of anything.

On Your Toes was one of the most unusual musical comedies to open on Broadway in 1936, for it was one of the first to incorporate ballet into the plot. The book was by Lorenz Hart, Richard Rodgers and George Abbott, with music by Rodgers and lyrics by Hart and the breakthrough choreography by George Balanchine.

Originally Rodgers and Hart had prepared an outline for a motion picture script about a Broadway hoofer involved with the Russian Ballet while they were working in Hollywood in the early 1930s. They hoped Pandro Berman of RKO would buy it for Fred Astaire, but eventually the idea was sold to the Schuberts for a stage version with Ray Bolger.

The show opens on the Keith Vaudeville circuit with a couple of veteran vaudeville hoofers, Phil Dolan II and Lil, who have a typical vaudeville routine 'Two-a-Day for Keith.' They want their son, Phil Dolan III, to follow a different and more ambitious career – something cultural, they hope. So Phil III becomes a music instructor, explaining his interest in 'The Three B's.' Along the way, he meets an amateur female songwriter, Frankie Frayne, and they hit it off, even thinking of stealing away where no one can bother them in the hit song of the show, 'There's a Small Hotel.' But Phil is becoming more interested in ballet and meets and falls in love with a ballerina, Vera Barinova. Afraid that he will lose her, he oins the Russian Ballet and becomes involved in a production that is an absolute farce – 'La Princesse Zenobia' – based on the tales of Sheherazade.

This brings the ballet company close to bankruptcy, but a friend of Phil's gives him the scenario for a modern ballet – 'Slaughter on Tenth Avenue.' Out of desperation, the troupe mounts the ballet, with Phil and Vera as the main dancers. The performance is a success, The Russian Ballet is saved and Phil realizes he loves Frankie rather than Vera.

This was Balanchine's first experience on Broadway, and he did a tremendous job with both of his ballet sequences – 'La Princess Zenobia,' a spoof of classical dance tradition, and 'Slaughter on Tenth Avenue,' a spoof of gangster movies. 'Slaughter' was about a dancer and his girl who are fleeing from gangsters and hide in a Tenth Avenue cafe in New York City. It ends with the girl being shot and the hoofer being saved by the police.

In the Warner Bros. film of *On Your Toes* (1939) Vera Zorina played Vera. The plot was changed, and this time the American composer/dancer (Eddie Albert) was mistaken for a traitor by a visiting Russian Ballet company. Apart from 'Slaughter,' it was remarkably dull. The movie did retain the 'Zenobia' ballet but the hits from the stage show 'There's a Small Hotel,' 'Quiet Night' and 'On Your Toes' were heard only as background music.

James Cagney played Eddie Bartlett, a mobster, in *The Roaring Twenties* (1939). He was a returning World War I soldier who tries to earn a living as a cab driver, can't make it, and turns into a mobster. Finally, he begins to hit the skids and sacrifices his life to save the husband of the woman he loves (Priscilla Lane). It was not bad, toning down the violence and sentiment of earlier gangster films from Warners, and was presented in a semi-documentary style. Also in the cast were Humphrey Bogart, Jeffrey Lynn and Frank McHugh. The studio had a problem with the role of a night club hostess, first casting Glenda Farrell, then Lee Patrick, then Ann Sheridan and finally Gladys George.

And thus ended the 1930s at Warner Bros. – a decade that saw the studio rise to preeminence in gangster films, social consciousness films and costume dramas. Along the way, Warners also held its own in the field of movie musicals. Then came the Forties.

THE FORTIES

THE 1940S BEGAN AS A time of austerity. Because of World War II, Hollywood found itself with virtually no European distribution, and that cut heavily into the studios' income. Catering to the Latin American market turned out to be no substitute. Warner Bros. was becoming known as the 'San Quentin of studios' and continued the production of tight budget films that had started in the 1930s. Actors and directors often worked 14-hour days. The waste of time, manpower and money was a sin to Jack Warner, and he steadfastly denied his creative employees any veto power over what they would work on or in. Bette Davis was the only exception to this rule. Oddly enough, the studio's product improved during this decade.

Warner Bros. released a grand total of 45 feature films in 1940 and had a profit of over two million dollars. The number of movies made dropped slightly to 37 in 1941, the year that Steve Trilling, a casting director, replaced Hal B Wallis as head of production. That was also the year in which Gary Cooper won an Oscar for his work in *Sergeant York* and Mary Astor won the best supporting actress Oscar for *The Great Lie*. Profits zoomed to over five million dollars.

Yankee Doodle Dandy made 1942 a banner year for Warners. The film garnered three Academy Awards for the studio – best actor (James Cagney), best musical scoring in a musical picture (Ray Heindorf and Heinz Roemheld) and best sound recording (Nathan Levinson and the Warner Bros. sound department). The best musical scoring in a non-

Above: *Pat O'Brien as Father Duffy, James Cagney as a soldier and George Brent as Colonel Bill Donovan* – The Fighting 69th *(1940).*
Previous spread: *The finale of* This Is the Army *(1943).*

musical film Oscar went to Max Steiner for *Now Voyager*. Profits were up again – to over eight million dollars.

By 1943, Humphrey Bogart was earning $3500 per week for 40 weeks per year. Of course, his most memorable film, up to that time, *Casablanca*, won the Oscar for best movie of the year. Paul Lukas won the best actor Oscar for *Watch on the Rhine*, beating out nominee Bogart in *Casablanca*. Other Academy Awards won by the studio were for best director (Michael Curtiz for *Casablanca*), best editing (George Amy for *Air Force*), best musical scoring in a musical picture (Ray Heindorf for *This Is the Army*), best original screenplay (Norman Krasna for *Princess O'Rourke*) and best screenplay (Julius J Epstein, Philip G Epstein and Howard Koch for *Casablanca*). Profits stayed at about eight million dollars.

Warner Bros. profits slipped in 1944 to about seven million dollars, but the studio released only 16 feature films. Still, artistically it was not a good year. For the first time in 12 years not a single Warner Bros. movie was nominated for an Oscar.

In 1945 Warner Bros. profits zoomed upward again – to almost ten million dollars. And the studio went back into the Academy Award business when Joan Crawford won the best actress Oscar for *Mildred Pierce*.

Humphrey Bogart's salary was raised to $5000 per week in 1946. He had to make at least one movie per year, but he was to have his choice of three different scripts before he made up his mind. Profit took a gigantic leap to almost twenty million dollars.

Nineteen forty-seven marked the beginning of the Hollywood Communist witch hunts. Even so, Warner Bros. profits continued to rise – this year to over twenty-two million dollars. And some of the Warner Bros. Stock Company were in the big money, too. Humphrey Bogart was the highest paid male in the United States at $467,361, and Bette Davis was the highest paid female at $328,000 per year.

Warner Bros. profits slipped to about twelve million dollars in 1948. But the studio maintained the quality of their films. Jane Wyman won the Oscar for best actress for *Johnny Belinda*. Other Warners' Academy Award winners were Walter Huston for best supporting actor (*The Treasure of the Sierra Madre*), John Huston for best director (*The Treasure of the Sierra Madre*), John Huston for best screenplay (*The Treasure of the Sierra Madre*) and Claire Trevor for best supporting actress (*Key Largo*).

Although the studio made a profit of over ten million dollars in 1949, it was not a banner year for Warner Bros., since it was forced by a Supreme Court ruling to divest itself of its theater chains. Then, too, Ann Sheridan bought out her contract and left the studio and Bette Davis asked for her release and got it. Warners won but one Oscar that year – to Leah Rhodes, Travilla and Marjorie Best for their costumes for *The Adventures of Don Juan*.

The 1940s opened with the slam-bang *The Fighting 69th* (1940), a highly entertaining mixture of action and senti-

Below: *Edward G Robinson, as the research scientist, in his lab in* Dr Ehrlich's Magic Bullet *(1940).*

Right: *Edward G Robinson played the title role in* Brother Orchid *(1940). He is being congratulated by Donald Crisp.*

mentality presented at the brisk pace that marked virtually all Warner Bros. products. On view was a fictionalized tribute to the famous New York regiment, complete with portrayals of its leading figures – Pat O'Brien's Father Duffy, George Brent's dignified Colonel Bill Donovan and Jeffrey Lynn's poet Joyce Kilmer. But the picture belonged to James Cagney's fictional doughboy. In his unerring style, Cagney strutted, chopped out his dialogue in true tough guy style, tried to hide his fears behind a street bravado, endangered his comrades with his carelessness and finally, in one of those last-minute demonstrations of decency that so often marked his characters, heroically sacrificed his life for his fellow soldiers.

Dr Ehrlich's Magic Bullet (1940) was not only a fine film, but a courageous one. It told the story of the man who developed salvarsan – a cure for syphilis. Edward G Robinson was Dr Ehrlich, turning in his finest performance since *Little Caesar*, and the development of the plot was presented with good taste. Ruth Gordon was Frau Ehrlich, and also in the cast were Otto Kruger, Donald Crisp, Sig Rumann and Maria Ouspenskaya.

One of the happiest movies of the year was *Brother Orchid* (1940), in which Edward G Robinson was transformed from a tough mobster to a lovable orchid-growing friar. Also appearing were Ann Sothern, Humphrey Bogart, Ralph Bellamy, Donald Crisp, Allen Jenkins and Cecil Kellaway.

Ann Sheridan played a night club singer in love with a former plantation foreman, James Cagney, in the tropical comedy *Torrid Zone* (1940). In her second starring role, she stole the picture from Cagney. Pat O'Brien was the plantation owner, and the film was the eighth and last in which O'Brien and Cagney co-starred. They would appear together again briefly in *Ragtime (1981-Paramount)*.

Another Cagney-Sheridan picture was *City for Conquest* (1940). Cagney played a truck driver who turns prize fighter and Sheridan was his girl friend. Arthur Kennedy made his film debut as Cagney's sensitive musician brother. All three of them were sensational.

Pat O'Brien created one of the characters for which he is best remembered in *Knute Rockne-All American* (1940).

Less an accurate biography of the Notre Dame football coach than a flag waver for football and Mom's apple pie, it was a box office triumph. Ronald Reagan was also a hit playing the Fighting Irish star, George Gipp, and his death scene was rather moving.

One of the most startling opening scenes in the history of the movies could be found in *The Letter* (1940), in which Bette Davis empties her pistol into the man she loves. Also in the cast were Henry Stephenson, Gale Sondergaard and Herbert Marshall, who had played the lover in the 1929 silent version with Jeanne Eagels.

James Stewart and Rosalind Russell were the stars of *No Time for Comedy* (1940), an adaptation of S N Behrman's Broadway hit. Stewart played the part of a successful comedy playwright who longs to do meatier drama. The problem is that his first serious play is lousy. For some reason the movie was retitled *Guy with a Grin* when it was rereleased in 1954.

The posters read 'Towering thrills [in] the blazing mountain man-hunt for killer "Mad Dog" Earle.' The success of *High Sierra* (1941) hinged on the character of 'Mad Dog' Roy Earle of the John Dillinger gang. First Paul Muni turned down the role and then George Raft. Finally it was given to Bogart, who turned it into a personal triumph. It told the story of a fugitive who flees to the Sierra Madre and holes up with a variety of people – Ida Lupino, Arthur Kennedy, Alan Curtis, Cornell Wilde, Joan Leslie (as the club-footed girl with whom Earle falls in love) and Henry Hull. Lodged on a high mountain crag, this last of the great gunmen shouts defiance at the police below and is, of course, shot to death. *The New York Times* raved: 'As gangster pictures go, this one has everything

Above: *Ida Lupino tries to calm down Humphrey Bogart (playing 'Mad Dog' Earle) in* High Sierra *(1941).*
Left: *Ronald Reagan (center) played Notre Dame football star George Gipp in* Knute Rockne – All American *(1940).*

Opposite: *John Garfield, Ida Lupino and Edward G Robinson (as Wolf Larsen) in* The Sea Wolf *(1941).*

– speed, excitement, suspense and that ennobling suggestion of futility which makes for irony and pity.' The futility of crime was summarized by Henry Hull (as 'Doc' Banton) in a short speech to Earle: 'Remember what Johnny Dillinger said about guys like you and him; he said you're just rushin' toward death – that's it, you're rushin' toward death.' The film was a masterpiece because of the acting, the script by John Huston and the direction by Raoul Walsh.

The Strawberry Blonde (1941) was a delight from beginning to end. Set in 1910, it told the story of a dentist (James Cagney) who loses the strawberry blonde (Rita Hayworth) to a local contractor (Jack Carson) and then falls in love with her best friend (Olivia de Havilland). Ann Sheridan was to have been cast in the title role, but she was having a feud with Warner Bros. at the time. Also in the cast of this bouncy, appealing movie were Alan Hale, George Tobias and Una O'Connor.

The Sea Wolf, based on Jack London's novel, has been filmed no fewer than six times, but the 1941 version, starring Edward G Robinson, was the finest version of all. Robinson played the part of Wolf Larsen, master of the ship *Ghost*, who is a mentally disturbed martinet, picking particularly on the mild-mannered intellectual, Humphrey Van Weyden (Alexander Knox), whom he had rescued after Van Weyden's boat had been sunk in the Pacific Ocean off San Francisco. Larsen refuses to let Van Weyden off the *Ghost* and forces him to assume the duties of a cabin boy. A mutiny, led by a member of the crew, George Leech (John Garfield), is successful, and the film ends with Larsen and Van Weyden trapped on board the sinking *Ghost*. Others in the cast were Ida Lupino, Barry Fitzgerald and Gene Lockhart, but it was Robinson, Knox and Garfield who caused chills to go down the spines of the people in the audience.

Gary Cooper, in his 55th film, starred in *Meet John Doe* (1941), and it was one of his best. It was a timely picture that warned against the threat of Fascism. Cooper played a baseball player with a bad arm who is turned into a foil in a

publicity stunt by newspaperwoman Barbara Stanwyck. She teaches him to become 'John Doe,' the voice of the people, who will champion the cause of decency and fair play. The idea catches on, and John Doe fan clubs sprout up all across the country. Then came the bad part. The power-crazed publisher of Stanwyck's paper (Edward Arnold) demands that Doe suggest that he (Arnold) be nominated to run for president of the United States. Doe refuses, and the publisher exposes him as a fraud. The now destitute John Doe is about to commit suicide but is saved by Stanwyck. Also in the cast were James Gleason, Walter Brennan, Regis Toomey, Gene Lockhart and Spring Byington.

The wonderful warmth of *One Foot in Heaven* (1941) not only won critical praise, but also must have been a boon to the paper handkerchief industry. It was based on Hartzell Spence's biography of his Methodist minister father, whose turn-of-the-century movings from one church to another culminates in his finally being able to acquire a suitable organ for his last house of worship. Fredric March was spellbinding as the minister, striking just the right balance between piety and humanity, and Martha Scott was almost as good as his wife.

To say that Gary Cooper was effective in *Sergeant York* (1941) is an understatement, as is substantiated by the best actor Academy Award he received for his portrayal of the

Opposite: *Gary Cooper (left) played the title role in* Sergeant York *(1941). Here he contemplates his future with Ward Bond.*

Above: *Sterling Holloway shows Gary Cooper that he has become famous in* Meet John Doe *(1941). Seated left – Walter Brennan.*

Tennessee backwoodsman, Alvin York, who singlehandedly captured 132 German soldiers in the Argonne Forest fighting of World War I.

As good as they are, the scenes of the capture are not the most memorable aspects of the film. Where the picture really hits home is in Cooper's portrayal of a simple man who, after a hell-raising youth, is transformed into a religious pacifist who must, in a wrenching conflict with his sense of patriotism, decide whether to enlist or to stand as a conscientious objector. To that decision Cooper brings an unforgettable anguish.

Cooper's assignment to *Sergeant York* was not a Warner Bros. decision. For years, the real-life York, whose 1918 feat had won him the Congressional Medal of Honor, steadfastly rejected every Hollywood application – including one from Cecil B DeMille – to film his story. When York at last agreed to a Warner Bros. request, it was with the proviso that he be allowed to supervise all aspects of the production and that Cooper be assigned to the title role.

Happily agreeing, Warners then turned out a film that was criticized for the studio sets meant to pass for the Tennessee backwoods, congratulated for its realistic combat sequences, commended for its patriotic ardor at a time when America was facing a new war and applauded for the performances not only by Cooper, but by three of Hollywood's best character players – Walter Brennan, Ward Bond and, in the role of York's mother, Margaret Wycherly. Both Brennan and Wycherly received Academy Award nominations for best supporting performances.

One of Ronald Reagan's better roles was that of a cocky flier ferrying Lockheed bombers to Britain and joining the Royal Air Force in *International Squadron* (1941), which was a virtual remake of *Ceiling Zero* (1935), which had starred James Cagney and Pat O'Brien. Reagan's irresponsibility causes the deaths of two of his comrades and he has a change of heart and takes on a suicide mission.

John Huston, the scriptwriter, finally got to direct a film in 1941, and what a film it was. Jack Warner commissioned him for the third remake of *The Maltese Falcon*. George Raft was supposed to play Sam Spade, but he didn't want to work with a first-time director, so, as had happened with *High Sierra*, Humphrey Bogart got the part. Huston was given the standard gangster picture budget of $300,000, and the studio didn't know that they were financing a masterpiece.

The posters for the film blared: 'Today something mighty exciting is going to happen! "Killer" Bogart, a guy without a conscience, moves in on Mary Astor, a dame without a heart.' The story, based on the novel by Dashiell Hammett, has private detective, Sam Spade, in San Francisco, becoming involved with a beautiful but evasive woman in a complicated plot to gain possession of a fabulous jewelled statuette. The mystery is as thick as a wall, and the facts are completely obscure as the picture gets underway. But slowly the bits fall together, the complications draw out and a monstrous but logical intrigue of international proportions is revealed.

Also in the splendid cast were Peter Lorre, Barton Mac-Lane, Lee Patrick, Ward Bond, Jerome Cowan, Elisha Cook Jr and Sydney Greenstreet – 'the fat man' – who was making his film debut at the age of 61.

The critics and the audience went wild. *The New York Times* wrote: '. . . we had almost forgotten how devilishly delightful such films can be when done with taste and understanding and a feeling for the fine line of suspense. But now, with *The Maltese Falcon*, the Warners and Mr Huston gives us again something of the old thrill we got from Alfred Hitch-

Below: *A scene from* The Maltese Falcon *(1941). Left to right: Humphrey Bogart as Sam Spade, Sydney Greenstreet (in his first movie role), Peter Lorre and Mary Astor.*

cock's brilliant melodramas, or from "The Thin Man" before he died from hunger . . . It's the slickest exercise in cerebration that has hit the screens in many months, and it is also one of the most compelling nervous-laughter provokers yet.'

Bette Davis asked Warners to buy the rights for the George S Kaufman-Moss Hart Broadway hit, *The Man Who Came to Dinner*, because she wanted to star in it with John Barrymore. Unfortunately, Barrymore couldn't remember his lines, so the part of Sheridan Whiteside went to Monty Woolley, who had starred in the role (a thinly disguised takeoff on Alexander Woolcott) on Broadway. *The Man Who Came to Dinner* (1942) told the story of an overbearing dinner guest who remains in a small town Ohio household, that was supposed to be his one-night accommodation when he came to town to make a speech, when he breaks his leg falling on the ice on the doorstep. Others in the cast, dropping in from time to time, were Ann Sheridan as Lorraine Sheldon (a takeoff on Gertrude Lawrence), Jimmy Durante as Banjo (a sendup of Harpo Marx) and Reginald Gardiner as Beverly Carlton (Noel Coward). Bette Davis made the most of her role as Whiteside's secretary, Mary Wickes was hilarious

as a nurse, and Billie Burke and Grant Withers were suitably confused as Whiteside's unwilling hosts. Wisecracks and insults proliferated in what was probably the funniest film of that, or most other, years.

The Male Animal (1942) was based on the Elliott Nugent-James Thurber Broadway classic about a stuffy college professor whose wife is about to leave him in favor of a former campus athletic star and whose department head interferes with his teaching methods. Nugent directed the film, which starred Henry Fonda as the professor, Olivia de Havilland as his wife and Jack Carson as her aging jock.

The blockbusting musical biopic of the 1940s, and maybe of all times, was *Yankee Doodle Dandy* (1942), starring James Cagney as George M Cohan. The United States had just entered World War II, and the time was right for this flag-waving (literally) story of Cohan, perhaps the greatest composer and song-and-dance man in American history. Cagney played the part to the hilt, and danced up a storm to boot. It was probably the high point in his career, and it won him the Academy Award as best actor that year.

Cagney had been type-cast as a gangster in such gems as *The Public Enemy* (1931), but he was, in fact, a dancer. He started in show business as a song-and-dance man, and his first film, *Sinners' Holiday* (1930), featured him in that role. He was naturally graceful – even as a gangster he had a lithe

Below: *Monty Woolley (in wheelchair) was Sheridan Whiteside – The Man Who Came to Dinner (1942). With him are Ann Sheridan, Richard Travis and Bette Davis.*

Above: *James Cagney, as George M Cohan, explains his plans to S Z 'Cuddles' Sakall (center) and Richard Whorf in* Yankee Doodle Dandy *(1942).*

Right: *Ronald Reagan and Ann Sheridan in* King's Row *(1942). He has just lost his legs and uttered the immortal line – 'Where is the rest of me?'*

grace that was as distinctive as his fast, clipped speech. Cagney went on from *The Public Enemy* to play a series of tough guy roles in which he was rough on women, but the dancer side of him was always there. It surfaced when he played a producer of musicals in *Footlight Parade* (1933) in which he got to do some dancing.

Yankee Doodle Dandy was the best musical of the year and one of 1942's highest-grossing pictures. It was not only an affectionate, melodious biography of George M Cohan, but also a nostalgic evocation of a colorful era in the American Theater. But it was held together by the immense zest of James Cagney. It was laced with some of Cohan's biggest hits, such as the title song, 'Give My Regards to Broadway,' 'I Was Born in Virginia,' 'Mary's a Grand Old Name' and 'So Long, Mary.'

One of the best pieces of casting in 1942 was to star Errol Flynn in the title role of *Gentleman Jim*. Based on the life of James J Corbett, boxing's first heavyweight champion of the world under the Marquis of Queensbury Rules, the film was marred only by its invented love interest (Flynn and Alexis Smith). Flynn worked hard at the part and had Corbett's boxing style down pat – after all, the two men were remarkably similar in temperament, background and way of life. Alan Hale played his father, and also in the cast were Jack Carson, Ward Bond, John Loder and William Frawley.

Now Voyager (1942) is almost the quintessential woman's picture. Bette Davis played a New England spinster who becomes a fashionable woman of charm after her mother (Gladys Cooper), a domineering shrew, causes her to have a mental breakdown. The studio wanted Irene Dunne, but Davis had, as usual, her own way. Paul Henreid played the architect with whom Davis has a doomed affair. His most famous scene was the classic moment when he lights two cigarettes at the same time and hands one to her. The 1940s generation, having learned to kiss from the movies, now had learned a romantic way to smoke. Equally memorable was the final line of the movie where Davis tells Henreid, 'Let's not ask for the moon when we have the stars.' Also seen were Claude Rains as her psychiatrist, Bonita Granville, Ilka Chase, John Loder and Franklin Pangborn.

King's Row (1942) was a splendid film about a young doctor (Robert Cummings) at the turn of the century who sees his small home town revealed in all its pettiness and squalor. It was a sort of forerunner of *Peyton Place*, with the fates of many townspeople intertwined, but it had power and

a beautiful score by Erich Wolfgang Korngold. Turning in stunning performances were Ann Sheridan, Betty Field, Charles Coburn, Claude Rains, Judith Anderson, Maria Ouspenskaya, and, in his finest acting job ever, Ronald Reagan. He played the hometown boy who loses his legs and had the wonderful line as he regains consciousness, 'Where is the rest of me?,' a line he later used as the title of his autobiography.

The center of the action in *Casablanca* (1943) was Rick's Café Américain. The café is a combination bar, night club and gambling casino, presided over by Rick (Humphrey Bogart) himself. The pastry chef was formerly Amsterdam's leading banker, a member of the Free French underground wanders around wearing a ring that conceals a Cross of Lorraine, a black pianist named Sam sings and plays nostalgic tunes and the roulette wheel is set to stop at number 22 on command.

Rick is a tough fellow who is surprised when Ilsa (Ingrid Bergman), whom he had previously loved in Paris, shows up in his café with her husband, a fugitive Czech patriot (Paul Henreid). The Nazis are tailing the young Czech – the Vichy officials (led by Claude Rains) offer only brief refuge – and Rick holds the only two sure passports which will guarantee his and the girl's escape. Rick loves the girl, but she is married

Below: *Paul Henreid, as the architect, and Bette Davis, as the spinster, had an affair in* Now Voyager *(1942).*

to the other man and gets all choked up whenever the black pianist (Dooley Wilson) sings 'As Time Goes By.'

Eventually, of course, Rick does the honorable thing and gets his old flame and her husband out of the country on a plane to Lisbon. But along the way there were memorable scenes, such as Henreid's rising in the café while the Germans are singing 'Die Wacht am Rhein' to drown them out by leading the customers in the singing of 'La Marsellaise.'

Also in the cast were Conrad Veidt as the German Major Strasser, Sydney Greenstreet as a shrewd black-market trader and owner of 'The Blue Parrot,' Senor Ferrari, and Peter Lorre as the cowardly villain, Ugarte. Also in the film were a couple of Bogart's lines that went on to become classics – 'Play it, Sam' and 'Here's looking at you, kid.'

Action in the North Atlantic (1943) starred Humphrey Bogart as Joe Rossi, the executive officer of the *Sea Witch,* and Raymond Massey as its skipper. It was a story of a ship on the Murmansk Run during World War II and was full of action, especially when the *Sea Witch* was separated from the rest of the convoy during a German submarine attack. Indeed, the action was non-stop and harrowing, with the ship's crew knowing that if the *Sea Witch* sinks they will soon freeze to death in the icy waters. This certainly was one of the most rousing propaganda films of the war years.

Everything went wrong during the filming of *Edge of Darkness* (1943). Errol Flynn was going through his rape scandal. Ann Sheridan had just had a nasty divorce from George Brent. The shooting was delayed by fog in Monterey, California, and co-stars Judith Anderson and Ruth Gordon were trying to return to New York to appear in a production of *The Three Sisters* and almost had to be tied up to await the

break in the weather. The movie, which turned out all right after all, was the story of the brave men and women in a Norwegian fishing village who revolted against their Nazi oppressors during World War II.

In *Air Force* (1943), acclaimed as one of the finest US wartime efforts, Warners followed a Flying Fortress crew as it saw action in Hawaii, the Philippines and the Coral Sea. Directed by Howard Hawks, the picture featured fine characterizations by youngsters John Garfield, Gig Young and Arthur Kennedy and by character actors Stanley Ridges and Harry Carey.

Opposite: *The king and his castle. Rick Blaine (Humphrey Bogart) in front of his Rick's Café Américain in* Casablanca *(1942).*

Above right: *Humphrey Bogart, as executive officer Joe Rossi, plots the course of the* Sea Witch, *as skipper Raymond Massey looks on in* Action in the North Atlantic *(1943).*

Right: *Tail gunner John Garfield receives his weapon in* Air Force *(1943).*

Thank Your Lucky Stars (1943) was an all-star revue that Warner Bros. made in part as a contribution to the war effort. It starred Eddie Cantor, Humphrey Bogart, Olivia de Havilland, Errol Flynn, John Garfield, Joan Leslie, Ida Lupino, Dennis Morgan and Ann Sheridan, but Bette Davis stole the show with her rendition of 'They're Either Too Young or Too Old,' in which she lamented the lack of 'available males' who were all away in the war.

Dashiell Hammett rewrote Lillian Hellman's anti-Fascist play, *Watch on the Rhine*, for the screen in 1943. Paul Lukas repeated his Broadway performance as the anti-Nazi resistance leader, Kurt Muller, and won an Academy Award that year for it. Also from the New York cast were George Coulouris as a blackmailing Romanian count, Donald Woods, Donald Buka and Eric Roberts as Lukas' sons, and Lucile Watson. Bette Davis played a secondary role – that of Muller's American wife, Sara – and Geraldine Fitzgerald played the part of Coulouris' wife.

One of the most successful of the musicals in uniform was *This Is The Army* (1943), a super-duper musical that was a mélange of flag-waving, star-singing, fast-stepping showmanship tied in an unbeatable bundle of box office allure with 17 smash hit Irving Berlin songs. It made over eight million dollars for Warners and starred George Murphy, Joan Leslie, George Tobias, Alan Hale, Ronald Reagan, Joe Louis, Kate Smith and Irving Berlin himself. George Murphy, later to become United States Senator from California, played the father of Ronald Reagan, later to become President of the United States. Two of the most stirring moments were Irving Berlin appearing alone on stage in his World War I uniform and singing 'Oh, How I Hate to Get Up in the Morning,' and

the rousing finale – 'This Time Is the Last Time' – sung by a chorus of 350 soldiers dressed in battle gear.

Princess O'Rourke (1943) was a wartime comedy about a princess who falls in love with a pilot, causing a diplomatic furore. Olivia de Havilland was the princess and Robert Cummings was the pilot. Norman Krasna wrote it (winning an Oscar) and directed it, too. The supporting cast of real professionals probably saved the movie: Charles Coburn, Jack Carson, Jane Wyman and Gladys Cooper.

Warner Bros. ordered submarine commander Cary Grant and his crew deep into Tokyo Harbor in *Destination Tokyo* (1944). The film was notable for the understated way in which it handled the very human fears of the officers and men alike. In this vein, one scene was particularly effective. John Ridgely, cast as an officer assigned to temporary duty aboard the submarine, is embarrassed by the terror he feels

Right: *Fifty-five-year-old Irving Berlin, in his World War I uniform, sings his 'Oh, How I Hate to Get Up in the Morning' in* This Is the Army *(1943).*

Below: *Cary Grant addresses his crew in* Destination Tokyo *(1944). Among the men were John Forsythe, Alan Hale and John Garfield.*

during a depth-charge attack. He sheepishly admits his fear to Grant, saying that the expression on his face must surely be giving him away. Grant quietly replies that the man looks no different than anyone else on board.

Warner Bros. refilmed *The Desert Song* in 1944, starring Dennis Morgan, Irene Manning, Bruce Cabot, Gene Lockhart and Faye Emerson. This time the plot had been updated to reflect the changes brought about by the war. The Riffs are fighting against the Nazis, who are trying to build a road from Dakar to the North African Coast in 1939, but the Riffs are led by an American (Dennis Morgan) who fought in the Spanish Civil War. The Harbach, Hammerstein and Romberg contributions retained were 'The Riff Song,' 'Desert Song,' 'One Alone,' 'Romance,' 'French Military Marching Song' and 'One Flower.' 'Fifi's Song' by Jack Scholl and Romberg, 'Gay Parisienne' by Scholl and Serge Walters and 'Long Live the

Night' by Marlo Silva and Romberg were added to fill out the changed plot.

Mr Skeffington (1944) was another Warners weepie. It covered the years 1914-40 in the life of a vain society woman (Bette Davis) who only married Job Skeffington (Claude Rains) because he lent her brother a large amount of money. She is so irresponsible that she thinks that she can cheat on her husband just because she doesn't love him. Then she loses her looks in a bout with diphtheria. At the end, Job returns, blinded in a Nazi concentration camp, and can't see how ugly she is. She welcomes him back and all ends well. The audiences loved the picture and cried all the way home.

Starring Dennis Morgan, *God Is My Co-Pilot* (1945) told the story of 34-year-old Colonel Robert Lee Scott who, on being dismissed by the Army as too ancient for combat service, became a hero in Burma with General Claire

Right: *Joan Leslie played Julie Adams the true love of Robert Alda (as George Gershwin) in* Rhapsody in Blue *(1945).*
Opposite: *Humphrey Bogart and Lauren Bacall in* To Have and Have Not *(1945).*

Below right: *Joan Crawford, as* Mildred Pierce *(1945), hugs her thankless daughter, Ann Blyth.*

Chennault's Flying Tigers. The plot and the performances were on the pallid side, with the film making audiences sit up and take notice only in its battle and aerial sequences. As the title suggests, there was a spiritual undertone present throughout.

To Have and Have Not (1945) starred Humphrey Bogart, and it was obvious that Warner Bros., having had such success with the sultry and colorful locale in *Casablanca*, wanted to put him back in a similar setting. They chose the Caribbean island of Martinique. Bogart was a professional sports fisherman who trawls the deep waters of pro- and anti-Vichy lawlessness. Finally, because of the lure of a beautiful stranger (Lauren Bacall, in her first role), he lends his talents to fight the Vichy forces. Despite Bogart's impressive performance, almost as good as he was in *Casablanca*, and Hoagy Carmichael's portrayal of Crickett, the sweetly sleazy pianist, Bacall stole the show. *The New York Times* described her as a 'wistful bird of passage who moves dauntlessly into [Bogart's] life, [this] blondish newcomer is plainly a girl with whom to cope. Slumberous of eye and softly reedy along the lines of Veronica Lake, she acts in the quiet way of catnip and sings a song from deep down in her throat.'

Rhapsody in Blue (1945) starred Robert Alda (who later became known as Alan Alda's father) as George Gershwin. It was a sort of pulp-fiction story of the composer, but it came off more credibly than most other composer biopics, since it captured Gershwin's enthusiasm for his work and some of the inner conflicts he faced. It was loaded with his fine songs and featured an almost complete performance of the title work, 'Rhapsody in Blue.' Audiences left the theater grieving at the composer's untimely death at the age of 48.

Mildred Pierce (1945) turned out to be one of the greatest

soap operas in motion picture history. Actually, it was a highly literate story about a woman's rise from waitress to successful restaurateur. A subplot was introduced in the conflict with the daughter she indulges, lavishing her love on the child, which, of course, is not returned. Warner Bros. originally wanted Bette Davis, who turned it down, and then Barbara Stanwyck, who turned it down, and then settled on Joan Crawford, who won the Academy Award for it. The selfish daughter was played by Ann Blyth, and others in the excellent cast were Jack Carson, Zachary Scott, Eve Arden, Bruce Bennett and George Tobias.

Christmas in Connecticut (1945) was a real money-maker for Warner Bros., and it taught the rest of the country that Connecticut always has snow at Christmas time and that all the residents of that state live in Tara-sized mansions. Barbara Stanwyck starred as a columnist for *Smart Housekeeping* (there's a clever magazine name) who is talented in cooking, motherhood and housewifing. But in real life she isn't. Not only is she single, but also she is inept at household jobs. The publisher of the magazine (Sydney Greenstreet) doesn't know this and asks her to entertain a war hero (Dennis Morgan) at her home over the Christmas holidays. Stanwyck comes up with a solution, which is that she needs to find a fake husband, a baby and a cook in order not to lose her job. In the film Barbara Stanwyck displayed a real flair for comedy and carried the role off beautifully. Also in the cast were Reginald Gardiner (as 'the husband') and S Z 'Cuddles' Sakall as the cook.

Pride of the Marines (1945) was not only a strong film but also one of the better screen biographies ever made. In it John Garfield portrayed Marine private Al Schmid who lost his sight during the fighting on Guadalcanal. In its early moments, *Pride* has the look of a standard combat film as it concentrates on the Guadalcanal action. (The night-time sequences at this point, however, are anything but standard;

they are chilling in their depiction of tired, frightened soldiers staring into the darkness where an invisible enemy lurks.) Once Garfield is wounded, the picture changes its direction and becomes the story of his experiences – in a hospital and then at home – in adjusting to his new life. That story, never once devolving into sentimentality, handles those experiences with intelligence and compassion. In the presence of these qualities, the film is reminiscent of the sensitivity on view in the handling of Harold Russell's double-amputee sailor in *The Best Years of Our Lives*.

Pride of the Marines resembles *Best Years* on yet another count. Both films hit an optimistic, upbeat note in their treatment of adjustment problems. It is obvious that their producers understood that both could be of service to the several million veterans just beginning to endure, physically or psychologically, their own periods of adjustment to civilian life.

John Garfield, whose screen career had been built mainly of tough and cynical characterizations, did some of his finest work in *Pride of the Marines*. His innate toughness is present in his Al Schmid and enables him to meet the trials of his adjustment, but it never overrides the hesitations, fears, angers and frustrations engendered by his handicap. Rounding out the emotional portrait is his tender concern for the woman facing his problems with him, his wife, beautifully portrayed by Eleanor Parker with the sense of inner strength that has marked so many of her performances.

Both received some fine supporting work from Dane Clark (as Schmid's best friend) and sensitive direction from Delmar Daves. Writer Albert Maltz's screenplay was nominated for an Academy Award. For reasons known only to those who dream up movie titles, the picture was shown in Great Britain as *Forever in Love*.

The Corn Is Green (1945), based on Emlyn Williams' stage play, starred Bette Davis as a selfless English schoolmistress

Left: *Dennis Morgan gets some domestic first aid from Barbara Stanwyck in* Christmas in Connecticut *(1945).*
Opposite top: *John Garfield, as the blind Al Schmid, confides his feelings to sympathetic Red Cross worker Rosemary DeCamp in* Pride of the Marines *(1945).*

Opposite bottom: *Young Welsh miner John Dall gets help from his mentor, schoolmistress Bette Davis, in* The Corn Is Green *(1945).*

who takes a young Welsh miner under her tutelage and prepares him for a university education. The film was splendid, though an entire Welsh village, built in the studio, was less than believable. Cartloads of dirt were strewn about the set, 20 tons of grass were used for the meadow scenes, and smoke machines were used to provide the haze that surrounds the typical Welsh mining village. But everything else about the picture was perfect. Richard Waring had played the young man on Broadway and was scheduled to repeat his role, but he was drafted and John Dall got the part. In the fine supporting cast were Mildred Dunnock, Joan Lorring, Nigel Bruce, Rosalind Ivan and Rhys Williams.

Devotion (1946) was a romanticized biography of the three Brontë sisters in which, more often than not, fact was turned into fiction. Ida Lupino played Charlotte, Olivia de Havilland was Emily and Nancy Coleman was Anne. Joan Fontaine (de Havilland's sister in real life) was originally to have the role of Charlotte, but the sisters had begun their famous feud, and the studio realized that this casting would never work. Not that Warner Bros. was on de Havilland's side. She had had a history of fighting for her rights and therefore

was given third billing under Lupino and Paul Henreid, who played the Reverend Nichols, a curate who (complete fiction) was the object of both Emily's and Charlotte's yearnings. Arthur Kennedy stole the movie with his portrayal of the tormented brother Bramwell.

The plot of *Two Guys from Milwaukee* (1946) was ridiculous, but it didn't seem to matter. A Balkan prince visits the United States and finds a cab driver who helps him understand how the American common man feels about his country. The cast was the thing. Dennis Morgan played the prince and Jack Carson the cabbie, and in support were Joan Leslie, Janice Paige, S Z Sakall, Patti Brady, Rosemary De Camp and Franklin Pangborn. The movie was a complete entertainment, especially in the last scene where Morgan finds himself seated next to his dream girl, Lauren Bacall, on an airplane, only to have a dangerous looking Humphrey Bogart force him to move to another seat.

Humphrey Bogart was back again as a private eye – this time as Philip Marlowe, in *The Big Sleep* (1946). Based on the novel by Raymond Chandler (William Faulkner, of all people, was one of the screenwriters), the movie was directed by

Howard Hawks, who had it moving so fast and with so little concern for whether or not its complexities were grasped that at times it became incomprehensible. But that very complexity, plus its speed and its sophistication, made it a masterpiece. The plot was so convoluted and contained so many twists and turns, that during production someone asked Howard Hawks who had committed one of the murders, and Hawks wasn't sure. He asked William Faulkner, who didn't know either. So Hawks and Faulkner called Raymond Chandler, who told them 'The butler did it.' Hawks screamed back at him, 'You're crazy; the butler was at the beach house.' To this day, no one knows who committed that particular murder.

But it really doesn't matter. *The Big Sleep* is not serious. It has to do with a bunch of whores, pimps, henchmen, killers, blackmailers, gamblers, a debutante who sucks her thumb and uses dope, and an invalid general who holds court in his greenhouse, where Marlowe sweats like a pig. It also had Lauren Bacall, as the sister of the debutante, with whom Marlowe carries on an incredible conversation in which they discuss sex in terms of horse racing, which was pretty racy for the time, no pun intended.

John Garfield played a young concert violinist in *Humoresque* (1946) who is supported by a wealthy alcoholic patroness of the arts (Joan Crawford). As her gigolo, he becomes moody, and Crawford begins to feel the pangs of guilt. Finally he finds that music means more to him than the good life, leaves her, and she walks into the ocean to the strains of Wagner's 'Liebestod.' Oscar Levant and J Carroll Naish were around to prevent this film from becoming too maudlin, and the music was fine, especially when Garfield fiddled around. This musical trick would have done credit to the special effects crew of *Star Wars*. A hole was cut in the elbow of Garfield's coat and through it was passed the arm and hand of a real violinist to do the fingering. There was also another violinist to take care of the bow. And on the sound track was heard the artistry of the real Isaac Stern.

Cole Porter was portrayed by Cary Grant in *Night and Day* (1946). The music was the only worthy aspect of this fabricated biography. It is doubtful that the composer grew up on a magnificent horse farm. Magnificent horse farms are not usually found in Peru, Indiana. It is doubtful that he com-

Above: *Violinist John Garfield and his wealthy patroness Joan Crawford in a pensive moment in* Humoresque *(1946).*
Opposite left: *Humphrey Bogart and Lauren Bacall discover another body in* The Big Sleep *(1946).*

Right: *Monty Woolley, Jane Wyman and Cary Grant (as the young Cole Porter) in* Night and Day *(1946).*

posed the title song while at the front, wearing a full-dress uniform, during World War I. But the songs, of course, were great – even Cary Grant singing 'You're the Top' – especially Mary Martin's re-creation of 'My Heart Belongs to Daddy.' Also in the cast were Alexis Smith (who had been George Gershwin's love interest in *Rhapsody in Blue* the year before), Monty Woolley, Ginny Simms, Jane Wyman, Eve Arden, Victor Francen, Alan Hale and Dorothy Malone.

Robert Mitchum played a Spanish-American war veteran in the unusual western, *Pursued* (1947). He is bedeviled by the memory of his father's illicit love affair of many years before, and is out to find his father's killers. The film relied more on talk than action, except for the violent climax, and sterling performances were turned in by Mitchum, Judith Anderson, Teresa Wright, Dean Jagger and Alan Hale.

Life with Father (1947) was a winner all the way. It seemed to be made with real affection. Based on the long-running Howard Lindsay-Russel Crouse stage play, it was set in the

New York of the 1880s and told the story of the Day family and how they had to cope with their opinionated, sometimes blustery, father. The cast was wonderful, especially William Powell as the father and Irene Dunne as the mother. Also in the cast were James Lydon as the oldest son and Zasu Pitts as Aunt Cora, along with a young Elizabeth Taylor and an old Edmund Gwenn.

Although the posters read 'Men turned tyrant and women sold their souls to possess the gold in a mighty mountain of

malice,' that had nothing to do with the plot of *The Treasure of the Sierra Madre* (1948). Scripted and directed by John Huston and based on the B Traven novel, the film told the story of three American vagrants 'on the beach' in Mexico who pool their scratchy resources and go hunting for gold in the desolate hills. There are run-ins with bandits, a discovery of gold, but the real plot is about the encroachment of greed into the soul of man.

Humphrey Bogart was magnificent as Fred C Dobbs, the prospector who succumbs to the gnawing of greed. Physically, mentally and morally, this character deteriorates before our eyes, dissolving from a fairly decent hobo under the corroding chemistry of gold into a hideous wreck of humanity possessed with only one passion – to save his 'goods,' as he calls the gold dust.

Walter Huston was equally brilliant as Howard, the wise old sourdough. He was the symbol of substance, of philosophy and of fatalism, as well as an unrelenting image of personality and strength. Huston played the part with such humor and gusto, human vitality and warmth that he almost stole the picture from Bogart.

Also in the cast were Tim Holt as Curtin, the third member of the team, and Bruce Bennett, as Cody, a fourth prospector who tries to horn in on the operation. There was also a young Bobby Blake (later to be billed as Robert Blake) who played a Mexican lad who sells Bogart a raffle ticket. But the best job of acting among the supporting players was turned in by Alfonso Bedoya, as the animalistic bandit chief, Gold Hat, who at the end has his men kill Bogart in one of the most supremely cynical scenes in movie history.

The production of *The Treasure of the Sierra Madre* was an adventure in itself. Huston had wanted to make the film for years, but had to wait until he came back from the Army, where he had honed his craft in making documentary movies. He wrote a screenplay and mailed it to B Traven, the recluse who had written the original novel. Traven wrote back a long letter and asked Huston to meet with him at the Hotel Reforma in Mexico City. After waiting there for several days, Huston was ready to go back to Hollywood when he was approached by a stranger who handed him a card which read 'H Croves, translator, Acapulco' and a note from Traven that said, 'This man knows my work better than I do.' Huston hired Croves as technical advisor on the film, and was puzzled when Croves never would allow himself to be photographed. After the picture was made, Huston somehow came upon a rare picture of Traven. It was Croves. And Huston never saw the man again.

Treasure was one of the first postwar films to be shot entirely on location, and the shooting was difficult and the conditions primitive. While Huston was casting extras, he was informed that the price was ten pesos a day, but if he were to pay 50 pesos a day, he could shoot them in an arm or a leg. However, they were not to be killed.

Many of the moments in the picture have since become classics: the gold dust being blown back into the hills where it was so laboriously mined; the killing of Fred C Dobbs; the glint in Humphrey Bogart's eyes as Walter Huston weighs out the gold; the night that the three adventurers decide that each man will guard his own 'goods'; Walter Huston's trusting look back as he is being taken off by peaceful Indians; Gold Hat's shadow when he appears behind Dobbs at the water

Peaceful Mexicans seek help from Walter Huston, Humphrey Bogart and Tim Holt in The Treasure of the Sierra Madre *(1948).*

hole. But best of all was the ending when Gold Hat and his bandits go into town to sell Dobbs' burros. Someone spots a brand on the burros, a boy runs to the police, the people in the market place stall the thieves, surround them and then turn them over to the Federales for immediate execution. The sequence lasts for nearly a whole reel and the entire dialogue is in Spanish. It is a tribute to John Huston's screenplay that, although no English is spoken, every moment is comprehensible. Huston was telling his story visually, at the very highest level of screen art. He deserved his two Academy Awards, as best director and screenwriter, as did his father, Walter Huston, as best supporting actor.

Johnny Belinda (1948) won a best actress Oscar for Jane Wyman, who played the deaf-mute victim, heartlessly called 'the Dummy,' of a rape. Her performance was heart-breaking in its conviction. Charles Bickford played her martinet fisherman father, Agnes Moorhead was her tough but kind aunt and Lew Ayres was the doctor who becomes her protector after she gives birth to her child ('Johnny Belinda') and then shoots and kills the rapist (Stephen McNally). Wyman had been at Warner Bros. for more than ten years without ever being given a decent part, so she had struck out on her own. After giving fine performances, such as in *The Lost Weekend* (1945 at Paramount) and *The Yearling* (1946 at MGM), she returned once again to Warners for this, her 28th and best film.

Based on a play by Maxwell Anderson, *Key Largo* (1948)

Opposite: *Jane Wyman, in her Academy Award-winning role in* Johnny Belinda *(1948), with Charles Bickford (standing) and Lew Ayres.*

Above: *Part of the all-star cast of* Key Largo *(1948) – Edward G Robinson, Humphrey Bogart, Lauren Bacall and Lionel Barrymore.*

told the story of a group of hoods who take over a resort hotel during a storm and bully the employees and the guests. The movie turned out to be a parable that taught that humans must fight evil in order not to find themselves in the clutches of a despot. This corny restatement of the dangers of totalitarianism was not needed by audiences that were just recovering from World War II, but the cast was so strong that people forgot the cliché and enjoyed the picture anyway. Humphrey Bogart was as effective as he had been in *Casablanca*, Edward G Robinson was as evil as he had been in *The Sea Wolf*, Claire Trevor was brilliant as the gangster's alcoholic moll (she won the best supporting actress Academy Award for the role) and Lauren Bacall was Lauren Bacall.

Rope (1948) was a most unusual film in many respects. First of all, it was Alfred Hitchcock's first movie to be shot in color. It had eight camera setups, each of which lasted a full ten minutes without cutting away from the action – giving the audience the impression that all the events in the picture took place between 7:30 and 9:15 in a single evening. The plot was inspired by the Leopold-Loeb murder case and told the story of two young homosexuals (John Dall and Farley

Above: *An aging Errol Flynn at the beginning of a duel with Robert Douglas in* The Adventures of Don Juan *(1949). Viveca Lindfors looks on.*

Right: *James Stewart confronts John Dall and Farley Granger with evidence linking them with a murder in Alfred Hitchcock's* Rope *(1948).*

Granger) who strangle a college friend for kicks and hide his body in a chest in their apartment in the very room that the dead man's parents and fiancée will be coming into for a cocktail party. James Stewart played their former college professor whose probing results in the disclosure of the murder, and Cedric Hardwicke gave a moving performance as the dead man's father. It was a flawed triumph, but it made a great deal of profit for Warner Bros., after the costs of $1,500,000 ($300,000 went to Stewart alone) were paid off.

Union problems with the studio's set designers had delayed the filming of *The Adventures of Don Juan* (1949) at Warners since 1945. By the time that production was started in 1947, Errol Flynn was in sad shape – his high living having caused a breakdown in his health – and the production schedule was prolonged, increasing the budget by a quarter of a million dollars at a time when the studio was making economic cuts. But Flynn was still a great swashbuckler, even at the age of 39. What plot there was involved Flynn, as Don Juan of course, saving Queen Margaret (Viveca Lindfors) and the king (Romney Brent) from the treacherous Duke de Lorca (Robert Douglas). Including an exciting climactic duel on a palace staircase, the film was a sensation in Europe but not too successful in the United States. It was obvious that Flynn's performance had been assembled from bits and

Above: *James Cagney learns that Edmund O'Brien is not a criminal, but a Treasury Agent, in* White Heat *(1949).*

pieces of film clips because his powers of concentration were on the decline, and he had to be photographed in such a way as to make him look more healthy than he really was.

White Heat (1949) was one of James Cagney's greatest crime dramas. The publicity department's blurb described his character, Cody Jarrett, as a 'homicidal paranoic with a mother fixation,' and Cagney played it to the hilt, especially in the shattering, yet convincing scene in prison where he learns of the death of his mother and goes berserk. It told the story of a killer who goes to jail on a minor charge to evade a murder rap. The ending was magnificent. Jarrett says good-bye to the world from the top of a blazing oil tank by shouting, 'Made it, Ma! Top of the world!' Virginia Mayo was properly sluttish as his wife. Steve Cochrane was Cagney's two-timing henchman and Edmund O'Brien was the Treasury Agent who worked undercover as a prisoner to win Cagney's confidence.

And so the 1940s were over for Warner Bros. – a decade of ups and downs, but mostly ups, as far as quality and profits were concerned.

THE
FIFTIES

WARNER BROS., ALONG with most other Hollywood studios, was forced to make a lot of changes during the decade of the 1950s. Television had arrived, people were staying home looking at the tube and the studios had to try to get them back into the theaters. The answer seemed simple enough – give them something that they could not get on the home screen.

So the early 1950s became the era of the gimmick – Cinerama, CinemaScope, VistaVision, Todd-AO. The problem, of course, with these wide-screen processes, was that the studios had to come up with movies that would fill the vast expanses of screen – movies that would use casts of thousands. Unfortunately, most of the epics were eminently forgettable. Some of the Warners' efforts were embarrassments – *King Richard and the Crusaders* (1954), *The Silver Chalice* (1954), *Land of the Pharaohs* (1955) and *Helen of Troy* (1956), come to mind, and these films have almost disappeared, not only from the screen and the tube, but also from the minds of movie goers.

On the other hand, there were many fine movies made in the decade that were small scale, often black and white, that gave the movie fans something that they could not get on television – adult fare. Warner Bros., for example, came out with such great films as *A Streetcar Named Desire* (1951), *Baby Doll* (1956), *Rebel Without a Cause* (1955) and *East of Eden* (1955).

The 1950s was also the decade of the collapse of the star system and the rise of the picture made on location rather than in the studio. Making a film in Europe, for example, gave the Americans working on it a definite tax break. The studios found that they had 'frozen funds' in Europe that could thus be used. Production was cheaper in Europe, and studio upkeep at home was reduced. By the decade of the 1960s, 30 percent of all Hollywood productions would be filmed outside of the United States.

With the collapse of the star system, many new, small production companies sprang up, and Warner Bros. was able to house several in their now-unused space. Alfred Hitchcock moved in, as did Burt Lancaster's Norma Productions, Charles K Feldman's Group Productions, Jack Webb's Mark VII, Sid Luft and Judy Garland's Tranconia, Doris Day's Arwin and John Wayne's Batjac.

Warner Bros. released 28 feature films in 1950 and turned in a profit of over ten million dollars. Even though profits slipped in 1952 to a little over nine million dollars, it was a distinguished year for the studio. *A Streetcar Named Desire* was nominated for ten Academy Awards and won four of them – best actress (Vivien Leigh), best supporting actor (Karl Malden), best supporting actress (Kim Hunter) and best black and white art direction (Richard Day and George James Hopkins).

Profits dropped to slightly more than seven million dollars in 1952 and fell to slightly less than three million dollars in 1953, a year in which Warners' only claim to fame was the Oscar for best song, 'Secret Love,' from *Calamity Jane* (Sammy Fain and Paul Webster). Things were better in 1954, with a profit of almost four million dollars. Out of the 21

Right: *Burt Lancaster romances a peasant wench in* The Flame and the Arrow *(1950).*
Opposite: *Richard Todd learns he is going to die and is comforted by nurse Patricia Neal in* The Hasty Heart *(1950).*

Previous spread: *James Dean (right) in his first movie role has a knife fight in* Rebel Without a Cause *(1955).*

feature films made by the studio that year, 18 were in color, but it was one of the black and white films that won the studio its only Oscar – Dmitri Tiomkin's score for *The High and the Mighty*.

At the Academy Awards, Warners did better in 1955, when Jo Van Fleet won for best supporting actress (*East of Eden*) and Jack Lemmon won for best supporting actor (*Mister Roberts*). In 1956 Warners got into the television business with both feet. They had had a great deal of success with a TV series based on one of their feature films, *Cheyenne* (1947), and decided to make four more Western television series – 'Maverick,' 'Colt .45,' 'Sugarfoot' and 'Lawman.' Jack Warner also decided to sell all the films that the studio had made up to 1949 to television for $21,000,000. In May, most of the Warners holdings held by Jack, Harry and Albert were sold to a group headed by Serge Semeneko of the First National Bank of Boston, but the brothers were made directors of the group, with Jack continuing as studio chief. Profits were about two million dollars.

Profits went up in 1957 to over three million dollars, and *Sayonara* won three Academy Awards, for best supporting actor (Red Buttons), best supporting actress (Miyoshi Umeki) and best sound recording. In 1958, a year in which the studio lost over one million dollars, Jack Warner was given the Irving G Thalberg Award for his services to the cinema. To close off the decade, profits zoomed to over nine million dollars in 1959.

The Hasty Heart (1950) was made in England in a co-production deal with Associated British Pictures. It told the story of a arrogant Scottish soldier in an American Army hospital in Burma who is unaware that he has but a short time to live. The nurse and the other patients know of his illness and forgive him his nastiness. The final scene was completely believable and quite moving, with Richard Todd summoning

all his dignity when he finds out that he is dying. Giving equally fine performances were Patricia Neal as the nurse and Ronald Reagan as a wounded American soldier.

Burt Lancaster swung from chandeliers, scampered across rooftops, leaped from balconies and demonstrated his skill with a bow and arrow in *The Flame and the Arrow* (1950), a Robin Hood-like entertainment. He played a peasant from the north of Italy who sets out to overcome a land-grabbing tyrant. There wasn't much of a plot, but the action was breathtaking and Lancaster showed the audiences that he had, indeed, once performed in a circus. Also in the cast were Virginia Mayo, Robert Douglas, Aline MacMahon and Nick Cravat, who had once been Lancaster's partner in his circus act.

There was no way that a great film could have been made from Tennessee Williams' delicate play, *The Glass Menagerie*, but Warner Bros. tried in 1950. Jane Wyman, however, as the crippled Laura waiting for her 'gentleman caller,' was touching and sensitive, and Kirk Douglas as the caller and Arthur Kennedy as the poetic brother were just fine. But the pivotal role of the mother was butchered by Gertrude Lawrence, the dazzling musical comedy star, who seemed to think that she was in a domestic comedy. Giving the movie an optimistic ending was also a terrible mistake, but it was a valiant effort.

No, No, Nanette was remade by the Warner Bros. studio again in 1950. This time retitled *Tea For Two*, it starred Doris Day, Gordon MacRae and Gene Nelson. The plot was utterly disguised. Doris Day is forced to say 'No' to every proposition, offer or question in order to win a bet whose payoff would be enough to finance, and star her in, a Broadway show. Most of the original songs were eliminated, but a great number of other golden oldies were substituted. Among the salvaged numbers were 'I Want to Be Happy' and 'Tea for Two' by Vincent Youmans and Irving Caesar and 'No, No, Nanette' by Youmans and Otto Harbach. Other songs

Above: *The famous fight on the merry-go-round between Farley Granger (left) and Robert Walker in Alfred Hitchcock's* Strangers on a Train *(1951).*

Left: *Doris Day and Gene Nelson were a stand-out song-and-dance couple in* Lullaby of Broadway *(1951).*

Opposite: *Sparks fly between Stanley Kowalski (Marlon Brando) and his sister-in-law, Blanche Dubois (Vivien Leigh), in* A Streetcar Named Desire *(1951).*

included 'Oh Me, Oh My' by Youmans and Ira Gershwin; 'I Know that You Know' by Youmans and Anne Caldwell; 'Do Do Do' by the Gershwins; 'Crazy Rhythm' by Caesar, Joseph Meyer and Roger Wolf Kahn; 'Charleston' by Cecil Mack and Jimmie Johnson; 'I Only Have Eyes for You' by Al Dubin and Harry Warren and 'The Call of the Sea' by Youmans, Caesar and Harbach.

The Enforcer (1951) was a hard-hitting thriller about a crusading district attorney and starred Humphrey Bogart. The plot was summarized by the Warner Bros. publicity department. The district attorney 'matched himself against a nation-wide network of killers-for-hire . . . and tore apart the evil dynasty that peddled murder for a price.' The movie was a classic crime story and Bogart was at his height. Also in the cast were Zero Mostel, Ted de Corsia, Everett Sloane, Roy Roberts and King Donovan.

Strangers on a Train (1951) was Alfred Hitchcock at his best. Two men meet accidentally on a train and arrange an exchange of killings. The strangers were played by Robert Walker, as a psychopath, and Farley Granger, as a tennis star. Laura Elliott played Granger's wife and Ruth Roman was his mistress. Walker was brilliant, but the picture was almost stolen from him by Marion Lorne, who played his doting mother. This was certainly one of the best thrillers of the decade.

Lullaby of Broadway (1951) had Doris Day playing a singer who returned to New York City to find that her mother, Gladys George, was a down-and out-chanteuse. The score included standards by George Gershwin and Cole Porter, but it was the usual Hollywood version of Broadway and life on the stage.

James Cagney was splendid as an alcoholic newspaperman in *Come Fill the Cup* (1951) who tries to shake his addiction after he is fired. At times maudlin and at times implausible, the picture was still riveting. Others in the cast were Phyllis Thaxter, Raymond Massey, Gig Young, Larry Keating, Selena Royle and Sheldon Leonard. This just missed being a very important film.

Marlon Brando received $75,000 to star in *A Streetcar Named Desire* (1951), based on Tennessee Williams' play. A couple of changes had to be made in the original story about the brutish Stanley Kowalski, whose wife's sister comes to visit them in New Orleans. The references to the former husband of Blanche Dubois (the sister) as being a homosexual were deleted, and when Stanley's wife, Stella, leaves him, her motivation was changed to her disgust with the way that Stanley had treated Blanche rather than, as was said by Blanche in the original play, to 'hang back with the brutes.' The cast was marvelous – Brando, Vivien Leigh (who won the Oscar) as Blanche, Kim Hunter (who won the Oscar) as Stella

and Karl Malden (who won the Oscar) as Mitch, Stanley's friend.

Gregory Peck played the lead in *Captain Horatio Hornblower* (1951), in an adaptation of three C S Forester Hornblower novels. It told the story of a nineteenth century British naval captain and his seagoing adventures against the French and the Spanish during the Napoleonic Wars. Virginia Mayo played the admiral's widow whom he eventually marries. Even with its fake-looking studio backdrops, the movie was an excellent swashbuckler.

I'll See You in My Dreams (1952) was a biopic about pop lyricist Gus Kahn that tugged at the heartstrings and set the feet tapping. Danny Thomas was Kahn and Doris Day was his faithful wife. Featured, of course, were songs for which Kahn had written the words – 'Ain't We Got Fun,' 'The One I Love Belongs to Somebody Else,' 'I'll See You in My Dreams,' 'It Had to Be You,' 'Yes, Sir, That's My Baby,' 'Love Me or Leave Me' and 'Pretty Baby,' among others.

Cary Grant and Betsy Drake (who were married at the time) starred in a delightful comedy, *Room for One More* (1952). They played the parents of five children, three of them their own and two adopted. The situations were the type that one might find in such a large household that was dominated by the children, and some of them were rather poignant, such as when the resentment of the adoptees was shown. Also in the cast were Lurene Tuttle and George 'Foghorn' Winslow.

Nineteen fifty-two saw the Warner Bros. release of *Retreat, Hell,* which detailed the fighting done by the United States Marines' 1st Battalion during the Korean War. The picture was given some good battle sequences through a nicely-coordinated combination of studio sets and newsreel footage, but would degenerate to nothing more than a standard

Left: *Gregory Peck, in the title role in* Captain Horatio Hornblower *(1951), has his crew clear for action.*

Below: *Cary Grant enjoys being besieged by his children in* Room for One More *(1952). At rear, Betsy Drake.*

combat yarn with standard heroics and more-than-standard characters, among them Frank Lovejoy's tough captain and Rusty (later Russ) Tamblyn's innocent youngster who wants to be a hero.

One of Warner Bros. hits of 1952 was a musical with a complicated history. Postwar Broadway audiences were ready for a musical farce, and they got it in *Where's Charley?* in 1948. The book by George Abbott was based on an 1893 play by Brandon Thomas, *Charley's Aunt*. The lyrics and music were by Frank Loesser, Abbott was the director and starring in the Broadway production were Ray Bolger and Allyn McLerie.

Two Oxford students, Charles Wykeham and Jack Chesney, want to invite their lady friends, Amy Spettigue and Kitty Verdun, to the university with the intent of proposing marriage. But the guardian of both girls, Stephen Spettigue, insists that they have a chaperone for the visit. Charley is expecting a visit from his aunt, Donna Lucia D'Alvadores, a rich widow from Brazil ('Where the nuts come from'), and he volunteers her as the chaperone. Meanwhile, Jack's father is in debt so deeply that he tells Jack to leave school and marry Donna Lucia. But Donna Lucia is delayed in Brazil, and Charley is forced to impersonate her in drag – black dress, gray wig, lace gloves and all. The widow does make an appearance at the end, but sizes up the situation and takes a false indentity. The boys win the girls, Jack's father wins Donna Lucia and his financial problems are over.

Bolger as Charley was terrific. His female impersonation was never camp, his dancing was flawless and in his big song, 'Once In Love with Amy,' he was able to get his audiences to participate in the singing of the chorus.

Another song from the show, 'My Darling, My Darling,' was number one on the radio show 'Your Hit Parade' for weeks. Other popular numbers were 'The New Ashmolean Marching Society and Student Conservatory Band,' 'Make a Miracle,' 'At the Red Rose Cotillion' and 'Better Get Out of Here.'

Bolger repeated his success in the film version of *Where's Charley* (1952), as did Allyn McLerie. The Technicolor movie, choreographed by Michael Kidd, was shot on location in Oxford, England, and, unusually, the Loesser songs survived quite intact.

One of the most pleasant films from Warner Bros. was *The Story of Will Rogers* (1952), starring Will Rogers Jr playing the part of his own father and Jane Wyman playing his wife. It was filled with warmth and affection and was based on the reminiscences of the real Mrs Rogers from the time she met Will in Oologah, Oklahoma, to the time that she said goodbye to him before he took off on the fateful flight to Alaska with Wiley Post. Also in the cast of this Technicolor film were Carl Benton Reid, James Gleason, Slim Pickens, Noah Beery Jr, Mary Wickes and Eddie Cantor.

Beginning in the early 1950s, a new kind of monster picture began to emerge – either a prehistoric creature or a normal animal that had been either freed from beneath the sea by an explosion or changed into a horrible mutant by atomic testing. One of the first of these monster films was

Below: *Frank Lovejoy (left), as the tough captain, prepares a lieutenant (Richard Carlson, in trench) for an attack in* Retreat, Hell *(1952).*

Opposite: *Ray Bolger played Charles Wykeham, here masquerading as his Brazilian aunt Donna Lucia in* Where's Charley? *(1952).*

Above: *Kathryn Grayson and Gordon Macrae were the stars of the 1953 Warner Bros. remake of* The Desert Song.
Opposite: *Vincent Price, as the crazed owner of a wax museum, investigates the skills of one of his sculptors, Paul Picerni, in* House of Wax *(1953).*

Left: *Police prepare to battle* The Beast from 20,000 Fathoms *(1953). Here comes the rhedosaurus.*

Warner Bros.' *The Beast from 20,000 Fathoms* (1953), whose most distinguishing feature was the work of Ray Harryhausen, the American trick-film specialist and model maker. It concerned a dinosaur which is awakened from its sleep by atomic testing. It was called a rhedosaurus – part brontosaurus and part tyranosaurus, and it comes out of the sea to answer a mating call. But it turns out that its mate is a lighthouse whose call is a foghorn (the producers were serious). The creature is naturally miffed, destroys the lighthouse and runs to a Coney Island amusement park, which it also destroys. Finally, the poor beast is killed by a radioactive bullet fired by Lee Van Cleef.

Trouble Along the Way (1953) twinkled along the way. Charles Coburn played the rector of St Anthony's College and found that he needed $170,000 in order to keep the school going. The answer was to hire a top-notch football coach to create a money-making team. John Wayne filled the bill, although he was also a bookmaker, pool hustler and various other shady things. But he needed respectability to regain custody of his daughter. Needless to say, he fielded a winning team. Donna Reed was a probation officer, Marie Wilson was his ex-wife and Sherry Jackson was his daughter.

Warner Bros. brought out *The Desert Song* in yet another film incarnation in 1953, this time starring Gordon Macrae and Kathryn Grayson. This was at the height of the McCarthy

Era, and the hero could no longer be referred to as The Red Shadow. In further plot changes, this time he saves the French garrison from the evil Sheik Youssef (Raymond Massey) and wins the general's daughter. In addition to the classic Sigmund Romberg-Oscar Hammerstein II score, including 'Desert Song,' 'Long Live the Night,' 'The Riff Song,' 'Romance,' 'One Alone' and 'One Flower,' a song by Jack Scholl and Serge Walters, 'Gay Parisienne,' was added.

The posters read: 'The **Big 3-D** Feature You've Been Waiting For! In Natural Vision 3 Dimension and Introducing The Phenomenal Merger of 3-D Color! 3-D Action! and 3-D Sound! Half man, Half-monster – Stalking the show world's beauties he craves for his Chamber of Horrors.' They were talking about Vincent Price in *House of Wax* (1953). It was the old story of the disfigured wax museum sculptor who coats corpses in wax to put them on display in his museum, and of course the whole thing ends with a monstrous fire in which the statues melt and reveal their true selves. Warners had made a similar film, *The Mystery of the Wax Museum* in 1933. But it was the first major venture in 3-D, and it started a minor revolution that soon petered out. Price was properly sinister, Phyllis Kirk was properly frightened and Frank Lovejoy, as a detective, was properly baffled. Everyone loved it but the critics. The critics were not enthusiastic. One called it 'as wild a display of noise and nonsense as has rattled a movie screen

in years, [it] may cause a dazed and deafened viewer, amazed and bewildered, to inquire in wonder and genuine trepidation: 'What hath the Warner Brothers wrought?'

Alfred Hitchcock scored again in *Dial M for Murder* (1953) by sticking to the theatrical aspects of the original play and confining most of the action to a few rooms. It told the story of a tennis player (what was this thing that Hitchcock had for tennis players?), played by Ray Milland, who hires a killer to try to do away with his wife, played by Grace Kelly, in order to inherit her fortune. Also in the cast were Robert Cummings and John Williams. Although shot in 3-D, it was seen almost everywhere in its flat version.

It was long thought that CinemaScope could be used only in broad expanses of sweeping melodramas amass with casts of thousands, but *The High and The Mighty* (1954) proved that it could be effective in closed spaces. This film was one of the first of the airborne disaster movies in which an assortment of passengers on a flight between Honolulu and San Francisco have an emotional catharsis when the plane loses an engine. Robert Stack played the pilot and John Wayne the co-pilot who saves the day. The passengers included Laraine Day and John Howard as a married couple planning divorce, Robert Newton as a theater producer, David Brian as a cowardly playboy, Paul Kelly as a scientist and Claire Trevor

Above: *Robert Cummings tries to comfort a distraught Grace Kelly, who has killed her attacker in* Dial M For Murder *(1953). John Williams as Inspector Hubbard looks on.*
Opposite top: *Fess Parker (in robe) tells his horror story in* Them! *(1954), while Joan Weldon and James Arness (right) look on.*

Right: *Robert Newton (left) and John Wayne struggle with a stubborn door on the aircraft in* The High and the Mighty *(1954).*

as a jaded woman. It was a sort of *Grand Hotel* that took wings, and Big John was quite good whistling Dmitri Tiomkin's Academy Award-winning title song.

Warner Bros. was in the monster business again with *Them!* (1954), which featured ants who were mutated by atom tests on the desert. The desert sequences were eerie, and the ending, set in the Los Angeles sewer system, was scary. It starred Edmund Gwenn, James Whitmore and James Arness. Director Gordon Douglas said about it: 'I asked the [film] editor: "How does it look?" And he said: "Fine." I said: "Does it look honest?" He said: "As honest as twelve-foot ants can look."'

Them! was one of the better, if not the best, of the giant monster films and was the first to use atomic radiation as the rationale for its oversized creatures. It benefitted from a taut, well-written script by Ted Sherdeman with an above-average share of humor and characterization. But before production started, Warner Bros. tried to sell the screenplay to another studio. And when production was about to start, the studio slashed the budget drastically. Despite Warners' lack of enthusiasm for the film, *Them!* was the studio's top-grossing picture of 1954. Audiences and critics loved it. *The New York Times* said: 'Perhaps it is the film's unadorned and seemingly factual approach which is its top attribute. *Them!* is taut science-fiction.' And *Newsweek* raved: 'a right little fright of a picture.'

The picture that many Judy Garland fans remember as her best was made for Warner Bros., not MGM, her long-time studio. It was *A Star Is Born* (1954). It was also her last

107

musical. Janet Gaynor and Fredric March had made the original, non-musical *A Star Is Born* in 1937. It was the story of a girl's overnight success in Hollywood and the decline of her alcoholic star-husband. By the time that Judy made the film as a musical, the story had often been told, but it didn't matter because of Garland's musical genius and a fine supporting cast, especially James Mason, who was brilliant as Norman Maine, the failing drunken husband. Judy was at her peak singing 'The Man That Got Away' and 'Born In a Trunk.' And she was at her most winning singing 'Here's What I'm Here For,' where she sang, danced and pantomimed the woman in pursuit of the man. The music by Harold Arlen, Ira Gershwin and Leonard Gershe took the audiences' breath away. The advertising read '$6,000,000 and 2½ years to make!' It was worth the money and the wait.

After a four-year hiatus from film making, a nervous breakdown, a divorce and an attempted suicide, Judy Garland had staged a spectacular comeback. The premiere on 19 September 1954 outglittered anything that Hollywood could have invented for itself. The film met with rave reviews. But when theater owners found audiences balking at its three-hour length, Warner Bros. trimmed 30 minutes from its running time. The film leaped into the headlines again in 1983 when Ronald Haver, a movie historian, searched old archives for months and recovered the missing footage. The restored version again drew out the glamorous and the great and garnered new raves from film critics.

With one film James Dean changed from rebellious young Broadway actor to spokesman for the disenchanted youth of the 1950s. This was *East of Eden* (1955), based on the John

Right: *James Dean (left) again played a rebellious youth in* East of Eden *(1955), an adaptation of the John Steinbeck novel, costarring Julie Harris and Richard Davalos.*

Below: *One of Judy Garland's great roles was as Vicki Lester in* A Star is Born *(1954). Judy was at her pinnacle singing 'Born in a Trunk' and 'The Man That Got Away.'*

Steinbeck novel. Dean played Cal, the unloved son, always at loggerheads with authority. His was a powerful performance, and youngsters immediately made him a cult figure. Sanctification came later, when he died in an auto accident at the age of 24. The rest of the cast was excellent, too – Julie Harris, Raymond Massey, Burl Ives and Jo Van Fleet in her Academy Award-winning performance as Dean's mother. This emotionally overwhelming picture about two brothers' rivalry for the love of their father affects today's generation as much as

those who witnessed Dean's starring debut more than 30 years ago.

Mister Roberts (1955) had been a smash Broadway play about life on a small naval cargo ship floating 'somewhere between the Islands of Tedium and Ennui' in the Pacific Ocean – a play that combined comedy, poignancy and tragedy so effectively that those who saw it never forgot it. John Ford, the director of Warner Bros. film adaptation, insisted that Henry Fonda play the title role, which he had

109

Above: Mister Roberts *(1955)* – *Jack Lemmon as Ensign Pulver (he won an Oscar), James Cagney as the captain, Henry Fonda as Mister Roberts and* *William Powell as Doc Daneeka.*
Below left: *James Dean in* Rebel Without a Cause *(1955), his second film.*

created on the New York stage, even though Jack Warner had wanted William Holden. Fonda was signed, but a feud between Warner and Ford began, and Ford was replaced as director by Mervyn LeRoy. Fonda was excellent as the gentle cargo officer who protects his men from the tyrannical captain (James Cagney). Also in the cast were Jack Lemmon in his Academy Award-winning role as Ensign Pulver and William Powell as Doc Daneeka. *Mister Roberts* was one of the best pictures of this or any other year.

James Dean cemented his hold on the youth of America with *Rebel Without a Cause* (1955). Again it was a story of alienated youth and their problems with their elders. Dean affirmed his status as an icon and Natalie Wood proved that she had graduated from being a darling little girl into an attractive young woman who also had great acting talent. Sal Mineo, as Dean's friend Plato, established himself as an actor, too. Unfortunately, Dean's parents, played by Jim Backus and Ann Doran, were treated as caricatures.

The Court-Martial of Billy Mitchell (1955) saw Gary Cooper's interpretation of the World War I flier and visionary Army general who, in the 1920s, urged the United States to develop an Air Force independent of Navy or Army control.

Mitchell's broadly publicized view that the military was negligent and almost treasonable in its slow development of the nation's air power led to his 1925 trial for insubordination and a suspension from military service for five years. Mitchell resigned from the Army in 1926 and worked in civilian aviation until his death in 1936.

Cooper gave a thoughtful performance as the troubled Mitchell who stubbornly pushed the cause of air power and, in the process, so incurred the wrath of a reactionary general (solidly played by Charles Bickford) that the court-marial results. Joining Cooper and Bickford with fine performances were Ralph Bellamy as a congressman sympathetic to Mitchell's cause, Rod Steiger as Mitchell's defense attorney and James Daly as the prosecuting attorney. In all, though Mitchell's character was not as fully explored as Sergeant Alvin York's had been 13 years earlier, the film added up to an arresting and accurately-done courtroom drama.

Little Rhoda was a monster in *The Bad Seed* (1956). Played by Patty McCormack, the sweet little girl murders the classmate who beat her in a writing contest, and almost every time

that anyone thought that Rhoda was a murderess, he or she bit the dust, too. Finally her mother Christine (Nancy Kelly) realizes that the child who has inherited her evil genes from her own mother, a convicted murderess, must be destroyed. Also in the cast were Eileen Heckart and Henry Jones, who had appeared with Kelly and McCormack on Broadway in the original play. Of course, the Johnston Office (Eric Johnston had succeeded censor Will Hays in 1945) insisted that the girl die as punishment for her sins, although in the play ironically she is saved when neighbors hear the shot that Christine has used to end her own life after giving Rhoda an overdose of sleeping pills. But Mervyn LeRoy, the director, sweetened her death a little by having his cast take a sort of curtain call at the end of the movie, in which Nancy Kelly takes Patty McCormack over her knee and spanks her.

The Searchers (1956) was a rip-snorting Western that started with the tardy homecoming from the Civil War of a lean Texan and leaped right into a massacre by Comanches and the abduction of two white girls. And then it proceeded for almost two hours to detail the five-year search for the girls that was relentlessly conducted by the Texan, with the ultimate help of just one young man. Director John Ford created a film with a wealth of Western action that had the toughness of leather and the sting of a whip. The picture bristled with Indian fighting, tense, nerve-raking brawls between the

Below: *Gary Cooper as the idealistic Brigadier General William Mitchell in* The Court-Martial of Billy Mitchell *(1955), in which he played the Army Air Force hero.*

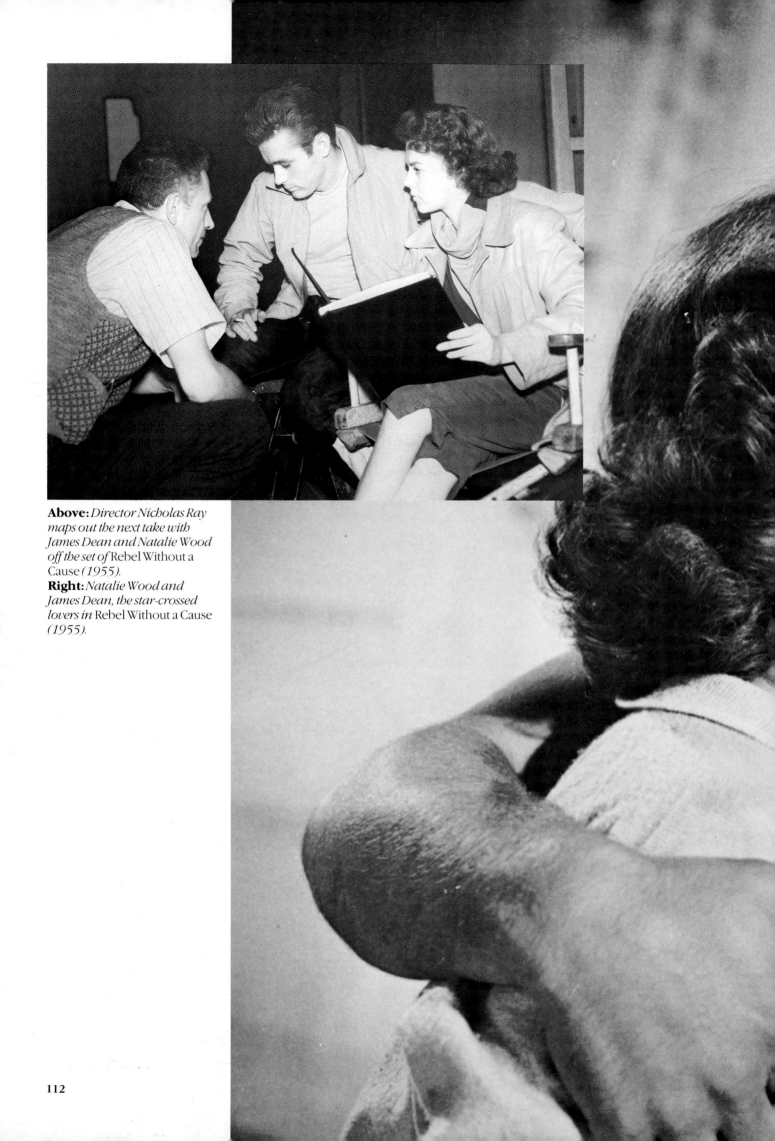

Above: *Director Nicholas Ray maps out the next take with James Dean and Natalie Wood off the set of* Rebel Without a Cause *(1955).*
Right: *Natalie Wood and James Dean, the star-crossed lovers in* Rebel Without a Cause *(1955).*

Above: *John Wayne returns home from the Civil War in* The Searchers *(1956).*
Right: *Leslie Benedict (Elizabeth Taylor) confronts Jett Rink (James Dean) in* Giant *(1956). It was Dean's last picture.*
Opposite right: *Gregory Peck played the driven Captain Ahab in* Moby Dick *(1956).*

Texan and his companion, and yet was laced with comedy. John Wayne was uncommonly commanding as the Texan, Ethan Edwards, whose passion for revenge was uncontaminated by caution or sentiment. Jeffrey Hunter was wonderfully callow and courageous as Martin Pawley, the young man who goes with him. Ward Bond was a dandy fighting parson, Captain Reverend S Clayton, in his plug hat and long linen coat. Also in the cast were John Qualen, Olive Carey, Vera Miles and Natalie Wood, in a stirring performance as Debbie Edwards, the kidnapped white girl who chooses to live as a Comanche squaw.

John Huston's version of *Moby Dick* (1956) was the best of all the productions of that complicated novel by Herman Melville. All the power and mysticism of that story about the obsessed Captain Ahab's attempts to seek revenge on the great white whale were kept intact. Huston had always wanted to do the film with Ahab being played by his father,

Walter Huston, but after the death of the elder Huston, Gregory Peck was signed to play the role. Richard Basehart was Ishmael, Leo Genn was Starbuck, Friedrich Ledebur was Queequeg and Orson Welles was Father Mappel. All turned in sterling performances. The picture was realistic, having been shot in Portugal, The Canary Islands, The Azores and Wales, which permitted the use of a real ocean and natural weather conditions. Indeed, the only things that were faked were the whales, which were made from latex.

Giant (1956) was a sprawling film taken from Edna Ferber's sprawling novel. It combined two stories in one. The first story was about the adventures of rich cattle baron Bick Benedict (Rock Hudson) who marries spoiled beautiful Leslie (Elizabeth Taylor). The other story was about Jett Rink (James Dean), a sullen Texas farmer whose life is changed when oil is found on his land. Others in the cast were Carroll Baker, Jane Withers, Chill Wills, Mercedes McCambridge, Dennis Hopper, Sal Mineo and Earl Holliman. This was Hudson's best performance, and Taylor's acting was near to her best. George Stevens won the Academy Award for his

Above: *Carroll Baker, in the title role of* Baby Doll *(1956), is caressed by Eli Wallach.*

Right: *Marilyn Monroe with Laurence Olivier in* The Prince and the Showgirl *(1957).*

direction. The picture became one of Warner Bros. biggest moneymakers of all time, netting $12,000,000.

Baby Doll (1956) was described as '*A Streetcar Named Desire* on *Tobacco Road.*' Written by Tennessee Williams and directed by Elia Kazan, the picture exhibited much of the personal conflict that was found in Williams' former play taking place among characters in an environment in which Jeeter Lester would feel entirely at home. Three of the four main characters were morons, or close to being morons, and the fourth was a scheming opportunist who took advantage of the others' lack of brains. There was Archie Lee Meighan (Karl Malden), the oafish owner of a broken-down country cotton gin, and his girl-wife, Baby Doll (Carroll Baker), an unmistakable victim of arrested development. Then there was Aunt Rose Comfort (Mildred Dunnock), an aged, pathetic simpleton, and there was wily Silva Vacarro (Eli Wallach), the 'foreigner' who runs a rival cotton gin. Vacarro discovers that Archie Lee has burned down his own cotton gin for the insurance. He finds this out while dallying with Baby Doll, who has never submitted to her husband, preferring to lie in her crib sucking her thumb. The movie would have gone down the drain except for the magnificent performance of those four actors, who somehow made all this trash believable.

A most unlikely pair of co-stars appeared in *The Prince and the Showgirl* (1957) – Laurence Olivier and Marilyn Monroe. Based on Terence Rattigan's flimsy play *The Sleeping Prince,*

it had Sir Laurence playing the stuffy Balkan prince who woos the gauche Gaiety Girl, Monroe. Dame Sybil Thorndike was the imperious mother of the prince, Jeremy Spenser was the prince's priggish son and Richard Wattis was a prissy minister. All of this was set in the Carpathian Embassy in London during the coronation season of George V. Oddly enough, it was Monroe's light performance that stole the show.

A Face in the Crowd (1957) was the sleeper of the year. In his screen debut (his only credentials were his starring on Broadway in the play *No Time for Sergeants*) Andy Griffith was a marvel as Lonesome Rhodes, the 'aw-shucks' hillbilly

Below: *Doris Day and John Raitt sing 'There Once Was a Man' from* The Pajama Game *(1957).*

philosopher and singer on a midwestern radio station, whose persona was manufactured, honed, and presented to the public by the media and who rises to the heights of entertainment power. Rhodes becomes the most popular entertainer in the country – everybody's friend – but inside he is a monster. He is undone when a supposedly dead microphone is actually on and his remarks about the suckers who hang on to his every word are broadcast. Also in the cast were Patricia Neal, Anthony Franciosa, Walter Matthau and Lee Remick in her first screen role.

Union problems in a pajama-manufacturing plant in Iowa was not the sort of stuff from which musical comedies or movies are made. But in 1957, Warner Bros. released *The Pajama Game*. The scene is the Sleep-Time Pajama Factory in Cedar Rapids, Iowa. The factory's manager and efficiency

expert, Hines, steps up operations in the plant, striving for higher levels of production. But the union is trying to get wage increases of 7½ cents an hour. Babe Williams is head of the union's grievance committee and presents the demands to the factory's superintendent, Sid Sorokin. Sid asks Babe for a date, but she tells him that they are on opposite sides of the fight and turns him down. Sid keeps at it, stealing a kiss at the annual factory picnic and calling at Babe's house. The raise is turned down by the factory's owner, and the workers decide to sabotage production by being careless and slowing down their pace. When Sid says that if things don't improve he will fire everyone, Babe kicks the machinery so hard that the plant breaks down and Sid fires her. But Sid is suspicious that the factory is making more than the owner lets on, and that he could afford the raise. To get evidence, he romances Gladys, the bookkeeper, who is Hines' girl, in order to get at the books. Sid reads the locked-up ledgers, gets his proof, the workers get their raise and Sid and Babe are reunited.

Some of the songs were 'Hey, There,' 'Hernando's Hideaway,' 'There Once Was a Man,' 'Once a Year Day,' 'Think of the Time I Save,' 'I'll Never Be Jealous Again,' 'Steam Heat,' 'Jealousy Ballet,' 'The Pajama Game,' 'I'm Not at All in Love,' 'Racing With the Clock' and 'Seven and a Half Cents.'

In the film version Warner Bros. proved that it was possible to transfer a stage musical to the screen without losing the zest of the play or making a stagey movie. Coming from the Broadway production were John Raitt as Sid Sorokin, Eddie Foy Jr as Hines, Carol Haney as Gladys and Reta Shaw. Doris Day was a good choice for the role of Babe, since she gave her most enchanting performance ever, managing to look both sexy and wholesome at the same time.

Above: *Marlon Brando and Miko Taka in an idyllic moment in a Japanese park in* Sayonara *(1957), based on James Michener's novel.*

Opposite: *Gwen Verdon as the seductive Lola sings 'Whatever Lola Wants' to Tab Hunter as Joe Hardy in* Damn Yankees *(1958).*

James A Michener's modern Madam Butterfly novel, *Sayonara*, described two international love affairs during the Korean War. When the film (1957) was released, Marlon Brando played a bigoted Army major who changes his attitude when he meets Japanese entertainer Miko Taka. The other set of star-crossed lovers were played by Red Buttons and Miyoshi Umeki, both of whom won the best supporting Academy Awards. Also in the cast were Martha Scott, Ricardo Montalban and the 29-year-old James Garner.

Damn Yankees premiered on Broadway in 1955, with a book by Douglas Wallop and George Abbott, based on the Wallop novel *The Year the Yankees Lost the Pennant*, and a score by Richard Adler and Jerry Ross.

The story concerned a middle-aged Washington Senator baseball fan who is turned into the young diamond superstar, Joe Hardy, by signing a pact with the devil and wins the pennant for the Senators.

The score included 'You've Got to Have Heart,' 'Whatever Lola Wants,' 'Two Lost Souls,' 'Those Were the Good Old Days,' 'The Game,' the moving love song 'Goodbye Old Girl' and 'Shoeless Joe from Hannibal, Mo.'

Warner Bros.' film version of *Damn Yankees* (1958) made only one mistake. Tab Hunter was cast as the young Joe Hardy, and he seemed to do nothing more than stand around with his mouth open, as if marveling at the talents that surrounded him. Apart from Hunter, all the main people

involved – actors, choreographers and writers – were recruited from the original stage musical, making this a most perfect marriage between Broadway and Hollywood. Gwen Verdon as Lola and Ray Walston as the Devil, Mr Applegate, were great; and remember that director George Abbott, Adler, Ross and choreographer Bob Fosse were the team that had also given audiences *The Pajama Game*.

Indiscreet (1958) was a feather-light comedy that seemed to be made for its co-stars, Cary Grant and Ingrid Bergman (Bergman displayed an unexpected subtle approach to comedy). Based on Norman Krasna's play, *Kind Sir*, it had suave banker-diplomat Grant telling actress Bergman had he is married, and then her discovering that he is not. That's about all, but it was a winner. Also in the cast were Cecil Parker and Phyllis Calvert.

Warner Bros. film version of *Auntie Mame* (1958), based on the novel and play of the same name by Patrick Dennis, starred Rosalind Russell in one of her most exuberant parts. Mame is a delightfully eccentric and boisterous woman of means who inherits an orphaned nephew, Patrick Dennis. The show spanned the years from 1928 to 1946. During the Great Depression, a time when Mame said, 'Life is a banquet and most poor suckers are starving to death,' she herself becomes destitute and then marries a wealthy Southerner, Beauregard Jackson Pickett Burnside. Patrick grows up and gets married. At the end, Mame is beginning to work her off-the-wall wiles on Patrick's son. Also in the cast were Forrest Tucker, Coral Browne, Fred Clark, Roger Smith, Patric Knowles, Peggy Cass, Joanna Barnes and Pippa Scott.

Audrey Hepburn, as usual, was radiant as Sister Luke in *The Nun's Story* (1959), which told of the spiritual problems of a nun whose vows of chastity, obedience, silence and poverty begin to become onerous. Sister Luke decides to become a nursing nun in the Belgian Congo, where she meets her Mother Superior (Edith Evans) and an agnostic physician (Peter Finch). His expressed views upset her, but lead her to reassess her way of life, and eventually she decides to leave her order. Also in the cast were Peggy Ashcroft, Dean Jagger and Mildred Dunnock. Colleen Dewhurst, as a homicidal patient, was electrifying.

The origins of Warner Bros. *Rio Bravo* (1959) were interesting. Howard Hawks, one of Hollywood's leading directors, didn't like the theme of the classic *High Noon* (United Artists, 1952), filmed by Fred Zinnemann several years earlier. He didn't believe that the citizens of any nineteenth-century Western town would refuse to help the sheriff protect the community, as they did to Gary Cooper in that film. When asked to make a Western the way he thought it should be done, he came up with *Rio Bravo*, which turned out to be a box office success.

In this story the sheriff of Tucson, Arizona, played by John Wayne, is threatened with attack by a gang of outlaws after he has jailed one of their members. Wayne is prepared to fight them alone, but many townspeople offer to assist him. Even Dude, his former deputy (played by Dean Martin), who has been on a two-year drinking bender, sobers up enough to help him. Another volunteer is an irascible old cripple (Walter Brennan). There is also a young gunslinger (Ricky Nelson) who is at first reluctant to get involved but does join up. The outlaws kidnap Dude and offer to exchange him for their jailed comrade, but Wayne and his helpers use guns and dynamite to rout the gang.

Besides taking the opposite tack of *High Noon* and still being a good movie, *Rio Bravo* was a turning point for John Wayne, who was established as *the* top Western star already, but who had played mostly serious characters. *Rio Bravo's* long story is filled with humor, and Wayne's character is gruff, tough, but also tongue in cheek. For the rest of his career, Wayne played characters with humorous aspects in many of his films.

The choice of Dean Martin to play opposite Wayne seemed unlikely at the time, but he gave a very good performance as a comic drunk and interacted well with Wayne. Ricky Nelson, another unlikely choice, was effective as the young gunfighter. Walter Brennan gave his usual solid performance as the ornery old-timer, and Angie Dickinson provided the love interest.

Rio Bravo marked a turning away from psychological Westerns in the 1950s; it was aimed purely as entertainment. And the director and cast made it so entertaining that it has joined the list of Westerns that aficionados call classics.

One of the first films based on a play by one of Britain's 'angry young men,' John Osborne, was Warner Bros.' *Look Back in Anger* (1959), in which Richard Burton gave a blazing performance as Jimmy Porter, a horn-playing working class candy stall owner who is disgusted with his way of life but can't do anything about it. He hates the drabness of the English Midlands, his failure as a husband, the Establishment and the fact that he can't make anything of himself. The mesmerizing Burton was ably supported by Mary Ure as his wife, Claire Bloom as his mistress and Gary Raymond as his best friend.

So ended the 1950s for Warner Bros. – a decade of highs and lows, but mostly highs. And good things were to come in the 1960s.

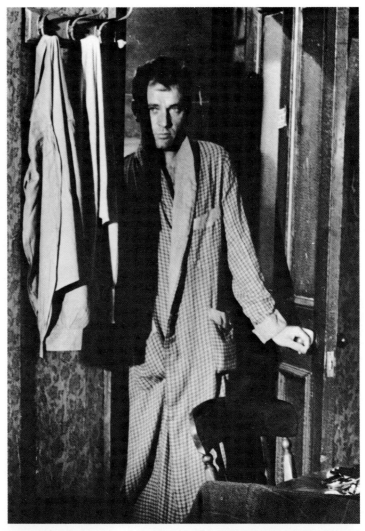

Below: *John Wayne shoots it out in* Rio Bravo *(1959).*   **Right:** *Richard Burton in* Look Back in Anger *(1959).*

THE SIXTIES

THE DECADE OF THE 1960S found Hollywood studios still in financial trouble because of the inroads of television. Many of them were forced to sell out to get financial assistance. Warner Bros. became Warner Bros.-Seven Arts Limited when it affiliated with a Canadian-backed enterprise. Then the company was bought by Kinney National, a company best known for owning a chain of parking lots.

Still, Warners turned a profit in 1960 of over seven million dollars. In 1961 came another Academy Award for best original screenplay – William Inge for *Splendor in the Grass*. And in 1962 the studio won two – Ray Heindorf for the best scoring in *The Music Man* and Norma Koch for best black and white costume designs for *What Ever Happened to Baby Jane?* That year the profits stayed above the seven million mark.

Gene Callahan won the Academy Award for best art direction in 1963 for *America, America*. And 1964 was a triumphal year that saw the studio winning seven Oscars for *My Fair Lady*: best film, best actor (Rex Harrison), best director (George Cukor), best color cinematography (Harry Stradling), best art direction (Gene Allen, Cecil Beaton and George James Hopkins), best scoring (André Previn), best

costume design (Cecil Beaton). But Warners suffered a loss that year of almost four million dollars.

In 1965, a lean year, Warners won but one Academy Award – for best sound effects – and it went to Tregoweth Brown for *The Great Race*. But profits held up at almost five million dollars. Artistically, 1966 was a better year, since *Who's Afraid of Virginia Woolf?* collected five Academy Awards, for best actress (Elizabeth Taylor), best supporting actress (Sandy Dennis), best black and white photography (Haskell Wexler), best black and white art direction (Richard Sylbert and George James Hopkins) and best black and white costume design (Irene Sharaff).

Albert Warner died in November of 1967, and never knew of the Academy Award triumphs his studio won for that year. For *Bonnie and Clyde* there were Oscars for best supporting actress (Estelle Parsons) and best cinematography (Burnett Guffy). For *Camelot* there were best art direction (Edward Carerra and John W Brown), best musical adaptation (Alfred Newman and Ken Darby) and best costume design (John

Below: *Sinatra, Martin, Davis, Lawford, Bishop* – Ocean's Eleven *(1960)*.

Previous spread: *Johnson, Oates, Holden, Borgnine* – The Wild Bunch *(1969)*.

Above: *Robert Mitchum and Deborah Kerr were sheep drovers in The Sundowners (1960), a film shot in Australia.*

Truscott). For *Cool Hand Luke* there was best original scoring (Lalo Shifrin). Warners' profits rose to over nine million dollars.

Nineteen sixty-eight's profits rose to over ten million dollars and the studio's Frank P Keller won an Academy Award for editing *Bullitt*. But 1969 was a disaster and profits slumped to a mere $300,000.

Ocean's Eleven (1960) was one of the first of the complicated 'heist' capers that were to become so popular in movies. It was a fun-filled tale of a group of Army buddies plotting to rob five Las Vegas casinos on a single night – New Year's Eve. Of course they couldn't hold onto the money after the successful robbery, but that was neither here nor there. The big thing was the scheme itself. The picture was charming and disarming and had an all-star cast: Frank Sinatra, Dean Martin, Peter Lawford, Sammy Davis Jr, Richard Conte, Cesar Romero, Joey Bishop, Angie Dickinson, Patrice

Wymore, Ilka Chase, Red Skelton and George Raft, the latter two playing themselves.

The Sundowners (1960) was filmed in Australia and starred Robert Mitchum and Deborah Kerr as sheep drovers – a married couple in the outback. Michael Anderson Jr played their son. It was an idyllic film, full of warmth and tenderness, in its portrayal of their itinerant lives, running into one person after another – the most memorable being the flamboyant Peter Ustinov. Among the other friends that they encountered were barmaid-innkeeper Glynis Johns, Chips Rafferty and John Meillon as sheep-shearers and Ewen Solon and Dina Merrill as the married owners of a sheep station.

Ralph Bellamy played Franklin D Roosevelt and Greer Garson Eleanor Roosevelt in *Sunrise at Campobello* (1960). The movie was based on the period of Roosevelt's life when he was struck down by polio. It began when the Roosevelt family was vacationing on Canada's Campobello Island and ended when Bellamy, on crutches, is able to stand to nominate Al Smith for president of the United States at the Democratic National Convention in 1928. Hume Cronyn played Roosevelt's friend and advisor Louis McHenry Howe, Ann Shoemaker was Sara Roosevelt, Franklin's mother, Jean Hagen was his secretary and Alan Bunce was Al Smith.

Fanny (1961) was based on part of the Marcel Pagnol trilogy and had a cast that included Charles Boyer, Leslie Caron and Maurice Chevalier. It was a gentle film, telling the story of two elderly men who want to marry a pregnant woman (Caron) whose lover has left her to go to sea. Boyer was Cesar, the owner of a waterfront bar, and Chevalier was Panisse, a sailmaker.

Elia Kazan produced and directed *Splendor in the Grass* (1961), the story of a sexually-repressed young couple in the Kansas of 1926. Cast as the lovers were Natalie Wood and Warren Beatty, who were magnificent as the Midwestern Romeo and Juliet. When their parents tell them that they are too young to be married, she goes insane and is put in a mental hospital and he starts seeing a floozy (Jan Norris). Also in the fine cast were Fred Stewart, Joanna Ross, Pat Hingle, Audrey Christie, Zohra Lampert, Sandy Dennis and Gary Lockwood.

In 1962, Warners released an adaptation of the unusual 1957 Broadway hit *The Music Man*, with book, music and lyrics by Meredith Willson. It was a happy-summer-day sort of

Below: *Hume Cronyn, as Louis Howe, massages the leg of the stricken Franklin Roosevelt (Ralph Bellamy) in* Sunrise at Campobello *(1960).*

Right: *Maurice Chevalier, as Panisse, the sailmaker, has an argument in* Fanny *(1961), a film based on part of the Marcel Pagnol trilogy.*

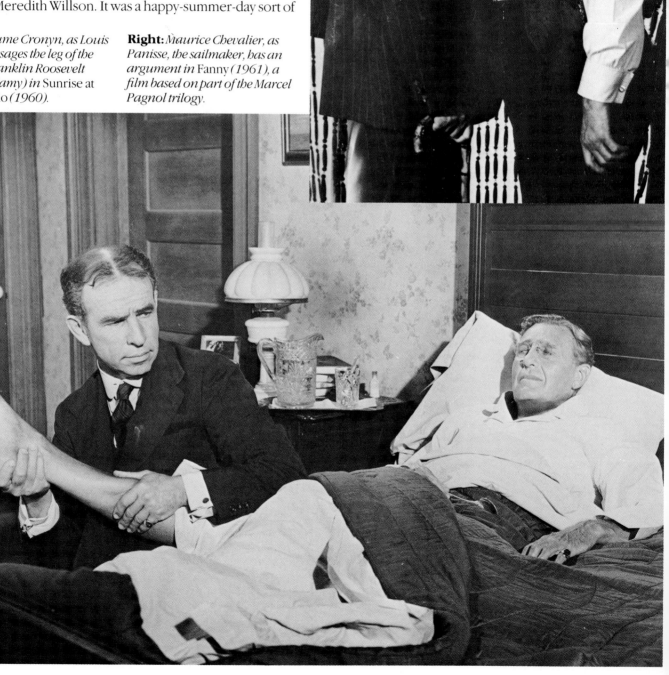

Left: *Robert Preston, as Harold Hill, and Shirley Jones, as Marion the Librarian, in* The Music Man *(1962).*

Above: *Natalie Wood was one of a pair of star-crossed lovers in* Splendor in the Grass *(1961), with Warren Beatty.*

musical about a con-man, Professor Harold Hill (Robert Preston), who arrives in River City, Iowa, to organize a boys' band, and, incidentally, to sell instruments and uniforms to all the kids. There he meets and falls in love with Marian, the Librarian, who reforms him.

From the startling opening, in which the audience felt they were aboard an old fashioned pullman car, to the ending where Hill turns honest, it had irresistible charms. Like the play the film wore its heart on its sleeve, but no one minded that sentiment often turned to sentimentality or that the comedy occasionally turned to corn.

Preston had been playing second leads in the movies since 1938, but this was his first musical, and he sang as if he had been doing it all his life and had steps that would have won first place in an old-fashioned dance contest. In short, he was superb, giving a lusty, vibrant virtuoso performance, and making one of the most sensational comebacks in theater history.

The fine cast also included Shirley Jones (replacing Barbara Cook) as Marian, Hermione Gingold (as the mayor's wife), Buddy Hackett (as a reformed con-man) and Paul Ford (as Mayor Shinn). Willson's entrancing score, which was made for whistling, included 'Seventy-six Trombones,'

'Trouble,' 'The Wells Fargo Wagon,' 'Gary, Indiana' and 'Pick a Little, Talk a Little.' For some reason, the beautiful ballad, 'My White Knight' from the stage show was eliminated and a new song, 'Being in Love,' took its place. Other hits were 'Lida Rose,' 'Marion the Librarian' and 'Til There Was You.'

The film also used an experimental technique of silhouetting figures before fading out at the end of key scenes. It was not a success, and not used again.

The stage show *Gypsy* had its Broadway premiere in 1959. Created by the same team who wrote *West Side Story* (book by Arthur Laurents, music by Jule Styne, lyrics by Stephen Sondheim and choreography by Jerome Robbins), this adaptation of Gypsy Rose Lee's autobiography starred the

Left: *Professor Harold Hill (Robert Preston) leads his band in 'Seventy-Six Trombones' in* The Music Man *(1962).*

Below: *Natalie Wood beginning her striptease as the sultry Gypsy Rose Lee in* Gypsy *(1962).*

earth-shaking Ethel Merman as Rose, the archetypal, loud-mouthed, fast-talking, pushy stage mother. The show also featured Sandra Church (as Gypsy) and Jack Klugman and ran for 702 performances.

It was a Cooks' Tour of auditions, backstage activities in vaudeville and burlesque and dingy hotel rooms. Gypsy began with a vaudeville act, 'Baby June and Her Newsboys,' managed by Herbie but actually controlled by Rose. Of course, Louise (later stripper Gypsy Rose Lee) is in the chorus of newsboys while her sister June stars. Meanwhile,

Above: *Natalie Wood, Rosalind Russell and Karl Malden in* Gypsy *(1962).*

Right: *Bette Davis (above) and Joan Crawford in* What Ever Happened to Baby Jane? *(1962).*

Rose has changed the act to 'Madame Rose's Toreadorables.' Herbie finds that he is in love with Rose and proposes, but she feels that she is much too busy for marriage. Vaudeville is fading, and Louise is faced with the necessity of becoming a burlesque stripper. She is a sensation, and the ugly duckling now has the nerve to quarrel with her mother. The show ends with their reconciliation.

After her performance in *West Side Story* (1961, United Artists), Natalie Wood was a natural for the part of Louise in Warners' film version of *Gypsy* (1962). She turned in a fine performance in what was possibly the best stage-to-film effort up to that time. There were, however, a couple of casting mistakes. Karl Malden was no Jack Klugman. But worst of all, Rosalind Russell (voice dubbed by Lisa Kirk) did not have the same kind of pizzazz as did the Broadway Rose, Ethel Merman. Russell wasn't bad – actually she was even good – but as one critic said, 'Where Merman had been volcanic, Rosalind Russell . . . was merely dynamic.'

Except for the deletion of the wonderful 'Together, Wherever We Go,' the film kept the score intact. Among the songs were 'Rose's Turn,' 'Some People,' 'Everything's Coming Up Roses,' 'Broadway, Broadway,' 'If Mama Was Married,' 'Let Me Entertain You,' 'Small World,' 'Baby Jane and Her Newsboys,' 'Mr Goldstone, I Love You,' 'Little Lamb,' 'All I Need Is the Girl,' 'Dainty June and Her Farmboys' and 'You'll Never Get Away from Me.'

What Ever Happened to Baby Jane? (1962) evoked the strange, unreal atmosphere of the Hollywood of the 1920s and 30s, even though the story took place in the 1960s. Bette

Davis and Joan Crawford played two elderly sisters who once had been movie stars, Davis as a child actress and Crawford as an adult temptress. Crawford was crippled and Davis was insane, refusing to realize that she was no longer the cute little thing that she had been. This was a real horror movie, in which the two, dressed in bizarre old costumes, battle each other for survival. A wonderful use was made of each star's early films to illustrate the movie careers of the sisters.

Elia Kazan filmed a tribute to his Greek uncle's pioneering spirit in *America, America* (1963). It told of the uncle's escape from servitude in Turkey and his arrival in America. It was a moving story of courage and determination and starring in the film was Stathis Giallelis.

PT 109 (1963) dealt with the naval exploits of a young John F Kennedy in World War II. Cliff Robertson, who was selected for the role by the Kennedy family, portrayed the future president in a film that won him praise for his work but that was judged to be slow-moving and poor combat fare.

If one takes a poll of one's friends and asks them, 'What was the greatest musical of all time?,' the answer is likely to be *My Fair Lady*. By now the whole world must know that *My Fair Lady* was a musical version of Shaw's *Pygmalion*, in which Professor Henry Higgins turns the guttersnipe flowerseller Eliza Doolittle into a proper lady, speaking correct English to win a bet. At any rate, the book and lyrics were written by Alan

Left: *Stathis Giallelis in* America, America *(1963).*
Below: *Cliff Robertson as John F Kennedy, hands the coconut message to a native in* PT 109 *(1963).*

Opposite: *Eliza (Audrey Hepburn) is disconsolate about her treatment after the ball, and Higgins (Rex Harrison) offers her a chocolate in* My Fair Lady *(1964).*

Jay Lerner, with music by Frederick Loewe. Directed by Moss Hart and choreographed by Hanya Holm, it starred Rex Harrison, Julie Andrews and Stanley Holloway. It ran for 2717 performances on Broadway and 2281 in London.

Rex Harrison was unique. He was the first non-singing actor to appear as a star of a Broadway musical since Walter Huston in *Knickerbocker Holiday*, and his rhythmical talking of the lyrics, his *Sprechgesang*, was sensational. Julie Andrews had been a star on the London stage at the age of 12, and here she was, the toast of Broadway, at the age of 21.

Many stage producers had wanted to make a musical of *Pygmalion*, but Shaw, remembering a former fiasco with his *Arms and the Man*, said no. 'After my experience with *The Chocolate Soldier*, nothing will ever induce me to allow any other play of mine to be degraded into an operetta and set to any music except my own . . . Hands off.' But when the 1933 movie of *Pygmalion*, produced by Gabriel Pascal and starring Wendy Hiller and Leslie Howard, appeared, he rather liked it. Of course he hated the ending. In the play, Eliza runs off to marry Freddie Eynsford-Hill and never returns to Higgins' Wimpole Street house. In the film she came back to

Above: *'Move your bloomin' arse' shrieks Eliza (Audrey Hepburn) to her horse at Ascot –* My Fair Lady *(1964).*
Right: *Henry Higgins (Rex Harrison) confronts Eliza (Hepburn), as Colonel Pickering (Wilfred Hyde-White) observes –* My Fair Lady *(1964).*

Higgins, and all he can say is, 'Eliza, where the devil are my slippers?'

After Shaws' death in 1950, Pascal asked Richard Rodgers and Oscar Hammerstein II if they were interested in turning the play into a musical, but they declined. So Pascal went to Theresa Helburn of the Theatre Guild, and she liked the idea. Helburn then talked, in turn, to Cole Porter, Leonard Bernstein, Gian-Carlo Menotti, Betty Comden and Adolph Green, and Lerner and Loewe about it and they all turned it down. Lerner later said, 'We had decided that *Pygmalion* could not be made into a musical because we just didn't know how to enlarge the play into a big musical without hurting the con-

134

tent. But when we went through the play again . . . we had a big surprise. We realized we didn't have to enlarge the plot at all. We just had to add what Shaw had happening offstage.'

The public had to wait eight years for *My Fair Lady* to appear on the screen in 1964. The picture had been in the news even when it was in production. Henry Higgins was again played by Rex Harrison, although the part had first been offered to Cary Grant. Grant, ever the gentleman, turned down the role, as he had done before with the role of Harold Hill in *The Music Man*, saying that not only would he not play the part, he would not even see the picture if Rex Harrison were not Henry Higgins.

Warner Bros. was suspicious of the charming newcomer Julie Andrews, and instead they cast Audrey Hepburn in the role of Eliza, with her singing voice supplied by the redoubtable Marni Nixon. Of course, Julie showed them when she won the Academy Award for best actress for her work in *Mary Poppins* (1964), another musical released the same year.

Harrison won the Academy Award as best actor for his work in *My Fair Lady*. The sets and costumes by Cecil Beaton were resplendent. The movie was sumptuously filmed. But much of the credit should go to the Alan Jay Lerner-Frederick Loewe score, with such memorable numbers as 'Get Me to the Church on Time,' 'Ascot Gavotte,' 'The Rain in Spain,'

'With a Little Bit of Luck,' 'Show Me,' 'I Could Have Danced All Night,' 'Just You Wait, 'Enry 'Iggins,' 'Wouldn't It Be Loverly,' 'Embassy Waltz,' 'On the Street Where You Live,' 'You Did It,' 'Servants' Chorus' and Harrison's splendid soliloquies 'Hymn to Him,' 'I've Grown Accustomed to Her Face,' 'Why Can't the English Teach Their Children How to Speak?' and 'I'm an Ordinary Man.'

Stanley Holloway was great as Alfred P Doolittle, Eliza's father, the dustman, but almost didn't get to recreate his Broadway role, for the studio had wanted James Cagney. The best surprise, however, was Audrey Hepburn. Audiences had been prepared to resent her, but she gave one of the greatest performances of her life. She justified the decision of the producer, Jack Warner, to get her to play the title role that Julie Andrews had so charmingly and popularly originated on the stage. It was Hepburn's brilliance that gave the extra touch of subtle magic and individuality to the film. One critic said, 'It is true that Marni Nixon provides the lyric voice that seems to emerge from Miss Hepburn, but it is an excellent voice, expertly synchronized. And everything Miss Hepburn mimes to it is in sensitive tune with the melodies and words.'

There was an interesting censorship problem while the film was in production. In the stage version, at the end of the Ascot sequence, the ladylike Eliza looses her sense of decorum in the excitement of the race, and, in her loudest and best Cockney, shouts at her horse, 'Move your bloomin' arse!' This was almost deleted from the film, but calmer heads prevailed and the shout remained. Had it been deleted, it would have seemed like history repeating itself. In the original non-musical film version of *Pygmalion*, another line had been deleted by the censors of the day – 'Not bloody likely!'

Who's Afraid of Virginia Woolf? (1966) was an adaptation by Ernest Lehman of Edward Albee's Broadway play and was an important cinematic breakthrough in terms of content and explicit dialogue. Basically, it was the story of a boozy confrontation between history professor George (Richard Burton), his wife Martha (Elizabeth Taylor), who is the daughter of the president of the college, and a young faculty couple, Nick and Honey (George Segal and Sandy Dennis).

Amid the bickering and shouting, the film dissected the love-hate relationship between George and Martha as well as the tensions that are building up in Nick and Honey's marriage. The whole cast was splendid, and Taylor won the Academy Award for best actress, as did Dennis for best supporting actress.

Warner Bros. returned to the depression years of the 1930s with *Bonnie and Clyde* (1967), with Faye Dunaway and Warren Beatty in the title roles. The picture portrayed the exploits of the Barrow Gang as a black comedy. The film was criticized for making heroes out of the gangsters and bank-robbers and for emphasizing blood and gore, but it did appeal to the nostalgia crowd and grossed more than $23 million in the United States alone. The final climactic scene, that had Bonnie Parker and Clyde Barrow being riddled by

Opposite: *Richard Burton and Elizabeth Taylor declare a temporary truce in* Who's Afraid of Virginia Woolf? *(1966).*

Below: *Bonnie Parker (Faye Dunaway) watches Clyde Barrow (Warren Beatty)* Bonnie and Clyde *(1967).*

machine gun bullets and, like marionettes, being jerked around in slow motion by the impact of the bullets, was harrowing. Also in the fine cast of this picture, which some critics cited as being the best American film in 25 years, were Michael J Pollard as C W Moss, Gene Hackman as Clyde's brother Buck, Estelle Parsons as Buck's wife Blanche (she won the Oscar for best supporting actress), Denver Pyle as a policeman and Gene Wilder as an innocent bystander whose car the gang requisitions.

It! (1967) was a strange film that was based on the ancient Hebrew legend of the golem. Roddy McDowall played a London museum employee who discovers a golem (Allen Sellers) in the museum's warehouse. He brings the monster to life and orders him to kidnap his (McDowall's) girl friend (played by Jill Haworth). On the way, the golem destroys the Hammersmith Bridge, and at the end walks into the water

and disappears à la Godzilla. McDowall is killed by an atomic bomb – rather like shooting a cannon at a fly.

It would seem that Audrey Hepburn is incapable of giving a bad performance. In *Wait Until Dark* (1967) she plays the part of a blind woman whose apartment is invaded by three thugs who are looking for a doll stuffed with heroin. How she outwitted the criminals was brilliant and had the audiences on the edge of their seats. The film, directed by Terence Young, was worthy of Alfred Hitchcock. Alan Arkin, Jack Weston and Richard Crenna were the thieves. Efrem Zimbalist Jr was Hepburn's mostly-absent husband and Julie Herrod was her 14-year-old neighbor.

In *The Frozen Dead* (1967) Dana Andrews played a mad scientist who finds a king-sized freezer full of frozen Nazis and revives them in hope of setting up a Fourth Reich. Also in the cast of this sloppy production were Anna Palk, Philip Gilbert, Kathleen Breck and Karel Stepanek.

Camelot had its premiere on Broadway in 1960. The book and lyrics were by Alan Jay Lerner, the music by Frederick Loewe. Directed by Moss Hart, with choreography by Hanya Holm, it starred Richard Burton, Julie Andrews, Roddy

Opposite: *Audrey Hepburn as the blind housewife in* Wait Until Dark *(1967), holding the fateful doll.*

Below: *Franco Nero, Richard Harris, Vanessa Redgrave – Launcelot, King Arthur, Guenevere – Camelot (1967).*

McDowall and Robert Goulet and ran for 873 performances.

The run was a fair one, and it had had a $3.5 million-dollar box office advance because of the success of *My Fair Lady*, Lerner and Loewe's smash collaboration. But it was not a runaway triumph. One problem was that it was based on T H White's *The Once and Future King*, a delightful trilogy which covered almost the whole life of King Arthur. And that was hard to cram into an evening's performance. So the text was not cohesive, the plot was not always clear and the humor was pretty weak. Also, and perhaps most important, there were not enough songs. In short, it was delightful to the eye and ear, but it lacked the unity and magic of *My Fair Lady*.

The songs were most pleasant, although they didn't exactly fill up the time. The numbers included: 'If Ever I Would Leave You,' 'Then You May Take Me To the Fair,' 'C'est Moi,' 'How to Handle a Woman,' 'The Lusty Month of May,' 'Guenevere,' 'What Do the Simple Folk Do?,' 'I Wonder What the King Is Doing Tonight,' 'Follow Me,' 'I Loved You Once in Silence' and 'The Simple Joys of Maidenhood.'

In 1967 Warners released the film version of *Camelot*. One critic called it 'an appalling film with only good orchestrations to recommend it.' Part of the problem was that the original Broadway cast was not in the movie. Instead of Richard Burton, there was Richard Harris; instead of Julie Andrews, Vanessa Redgrave; instead of Robert Goulet,

Franco Nero; instead of Robert Coote, Lionel Jeffries. Beside that, the picture was too long – one minute short of three hours. It also had too little of the wit of *The Once and Future King*. And let us hope that Harris and Redgrave were the last non-singers to be entrusted with major singing roles.

There were those, however, who thought that the movie had strong dramatic action, vivid characterizations and an intensification of the romantic interest that made it superior to the stage musical. Then, too, it cost a whopping $15 million to make, and the wonderful photography and settings showed it. Still, it was a costly flop, recouping less than half its costs.

As a sidelight, in one scene in the picture Redgrave wore one of the strangest costumes ever designed – a gown completely covered with pumpkin seeds stitched into the fabric. And the film contained one classic mistake. King Pellinore, played by Lionel Jeffries, first meets King Arthur about an hour into the movie, but 20 minutes before he was plainly visible at the King's wedding.

Harking back to a great Warner Bros. triumph, *I Am a Fugitive from a Chain Gang* (1932), *Cool Hand Luke* (1967) was an eloquent study of prisoners and prison conditions. Paul Newman was a psychologically disturbed loner who was picked up by the police for breaking parking meters. Sent to a prison camp, he becomes an unexpected hero when he

Left: *Richard Harris, as King Arthur, remembers 'one brief shining moment' in* Camelot *(1967).*

Opposite: *Paul Newman, as the parking meter attacker, digs ditches on a prison work detail in* Cool Hand Luke *(1967).*

wins a hard-boiled egg-eating contest. The film traced Newman's attempts to figure out why society is as it is, and was a tough, unsentimental drama. Apart from Newman's powerful performance, fine acting jobs were turned in by George Kennedy, Strother Martin and Jo Van Fleet.

Paul Newman made his directorial debut with *Rachel, Rachel* (1968), which starred his wife, Joanne Woodward. Both Newman's direction and Woodward's performance were splendid. Based on the novel 'A Jest of God' by Margaret Lawrence, the picture told the story of the loneliness of two middle-aged unmarried women in a small New England town. This poignant film starred Woodward and Estelle Parsons as the two women, and Kate Harrington as Woodward's aged mother, James Olson as the man with whom Woodward has an affair and Geraldine Fitzgerald.

The Green Berets (1968) was produced and directed by John Wayne and was released at the time when the American public's opposition to the involvement in Vietnam was reaching its zenith. But the film was an unabashed tribute to that involvement and an unquestioning acceptance of the United States policy at the time – in all, an ultra-conservative actor's chauvinistic statement that ignored the complex questions then plaguing the world. So subjective was the film's view, and so hot were the passions of the day, that it earned Wayne a ridicule he had never suffered before in a career that had

Above: *Paul Newman's directorial debut was* Rachel, Rachel *(1968), which starred his wife, Joanne Woodward.*

Opposite: *Colonel John Wayne urges on his troops in a Vietnam War battle scene from* The Green Berets *(1968).*

seen him become not just a film star but a national institution. And to make matters worse, *The Green Berets*, aside from its political stance, was simply an unsophisticated piece of war-film making. All the Special Forces soldiers under Colonel Wayne's command are undiluted heroes, courageous, selfless and dedicated. All the enemy Vietcong are heartless savages who fight dirty and set up horrible booby traps for Wayne's men, one of which is a spiked affair that takes easy-going Jim Hutton's life. The propaganda abounded even more than it did in the worst of World War II's offerings. Further, in the skirmishes and battles, though in true Wayne fashion, well-staged, had too much the smack of derring-do about them. And the settings were without the authenticity customary in big-budget productions: Much of the film was shot in Georgia – and looked it.

Bullitt (1968) might be characterized as a forerunner of the 'Dirty Harry' pictures of Clint Eastwood. The setting was San Francisco, and Steve McQueen, in the title role, played a police lieutenant who was being persecuted, not only by the Mafia, but also an ambitious politician (Robert Vaughn).

Above: *A segment of the famed car chase in* Bullitt *(1968).*
Left: *Politician Robert Vaughn (right) hounds police lieutenant Steve McQueen, who played the title role in* Bullitt *(1968).*
Top left: *Fred Astaire, as Finian McLonergan, sings 'Look to the Rainbow' to Petula Clark, as his daughter Sharon, in* Finian's Rainbow *(1968)*

McQueen's assignment was to solve the murder of a Grand Jury witness. The film also contained one of the best car chases in movie history, especially when part of the route was on that snake-coil San Francisco thoroughfare, Lombard Street. Jacqueline Bisset played Bullitt's girl friend, and also in the cast was Robert Duvall.

Still hoping to repeat the success of *My Fair Lady*, Warners produced one of Broadway's most whimsical and charming musicals, *Finian's Rainbow*, which had its premiere in 1947. The book was by E Y 'Yip' Harburg and Fred Saidy, with lyrics by Harburg and music by Burton Lane.

Finian's Rainbow was an odd marriage of an Irish fantasy

with a tale of social conflict. It involved sharecroppers, labor exploitation, racial prejudice, poll taxes, right-wing reaction and greed for gold. The setting was Rainbow Valley, Missitucky, where Finian McLonergan had brought his daughter Sharon. Finian plants a pot of gold that he has stolen from a leprechaun in Ireland there, because he thinks the land near Fort Knox might make the pot grow even more gold. Og, the leprechaun, wants the gold back, so he grants three wishes. The first transforms the bigoted senator, Billboard Rawkins, into a black evangelist, so that he will find out what it means to be black in the South. Og falls in love with Susan Mahoney, a deaf mute who speaks only through her dancing, and the

second wish restores her speech and hearing. The third wish secures Sharon's happiness with her boy friend, Woody Mahoney, Susan's brother. Finally, Og becomes a human being and wins Susan.

The score was excellent. Among the numbers were 'How Are Things in Glocca Morra?,' 'That Great Come-and-Get-It Day,' 'Look to the Rainbow,' 'Old Devil Moon,' 'When the Idle Poor Become the Idle Rich,' 'The Begat,' 'Necessity,' 'When I'm Not Near the Girl I Love,' 'Something Sort of Grandish' and 'This Time of the Year.'

Director Francis Ford Coppola was still pretty much of a neophyte when he filmed *Finian's Rainbow* (1968) for Warners. It was a self-indulgent movie, and Coppola later learned that camera tricks are no substitute for expertise. The picture was grandiose, and one never knew whether it was a romantic tale or a political and social satire.

Petula Clark played Sharon and looked a bit old for the part. Besides, she used her pop-singing style of slipping from note to note instead of using a musical comedy approach and hitting every note. Don Francks played Woody, and he and his voice seemed to fade into the background, especially when he sang 'Old Devil Moon.' Tommy Steele brought an out-of-place music hall style of acting and singing to the part of Og, and was completely miscast. But on the positive side, Keenan Wynn was properly blustering as the senator, and Al Freeman Jr was hilarious as a black inventor who tries to cross mint with tobacco to develop a menthol cigarette. The best things about the film were the choreography by Hermes Pan and Fred Astaire's dancing as Finian.

But, to be fair, the fault was not all Coppola's. The play had taken 21 years to reach the screen, and social-consciousness fantasies were out of date by the time the picture was released. Also, Astaire, good as he was as Finian, would have been much better 10 or 15 years before.

The violent Sam Peckinpah was responsible for *The Wild Bunch* (1969), which told the story of a group of middle-aged, saddle-weary gunmen who decide to do a final job robbing a railroad office near the Texas-Mexico border in 1913. Dressed as soldiers, they ride into town, rob the office and then find themselves ambushed by a gang of bounty hunters working for the railroad. A ferocious gunfight erupts, many innocent bystanders are killed, and the children of the town, who had just been torturing a scorpion, frolic among the dead and dying, mimicking death throes. The bunch is hired by a Mexican general, but, à la *The Seven Samurai*, kill the general and liberate the town he was persecuting. But in the shootout, they are gunned down. The film made violence look good. Every killing, and there were many, was made in slow motion with bodies flying and blood spurting. The posters read, 'The land had changed. They hadn't. The earth had cooled. They couldn't.'

Leading the Wild Bunch was William Holden, and the rest of the gang consisted of Ernest Borgnine, Warren Oates, Ben Johnson and Jaime Sanchez. Robert Ryan played the leader of the bounty hunters who pick over the bodies after the last showdown. Among his men were Strother Martin and L Q Jones.

Thus the violent decade of the sixties ended with a film perhaps all too much a product of its troubled time.

William Holden (left), the leader of The Wild Bunch *(1969), and Ernest Borgnine, as one of his men, dress in United States Cavalry uniforms to rob a bank more efficiently.*

THE SEVENTIES

THE BEGINNING OF THE new decade saw theater attendances falling once more. Ten years before, 43.5 million people per week had bought tickets to see movies, but in 1970, the number had dropped to 15 million per week. Still, people went to see what they wanted to see, and if a film was popular, it did well at the box office. This resulted in a few blockbusters and a lot of failures. It was during this decade that disaster movies came into their own, and the difference in right and wrong in a picture became clouded. Occult pictures flourished and violence blossomed.

Profits were up in 1970, to over twenty-seven million dollars. This was the year that Kinney reorganized itself as Warners Communications, Incorporated. But the company's only Oscar was for *Woodstock*, the best documentary. Profits in 1971 dropped drastically, to just over fourteen million dollars, and Jane Fonda won the Academy Award as best actress for *Klute*.

In 1972 the best original screenplay Oscar went to Jeremy Larner for *The Candidate*, but, perhaps more important, the Academy awarded an Honorary Oscar to veteran Edward G Robinson – 'who achieved greatness as a player, a patron of the arts and a dedicated citizen . . . in sum, a Renaissance man.' Profits rose to over twenty-three million dollars. Profits rose again in 1973 to over thirty-one millon dollars, and *The Exorcist* won two Academy Awards – for best screenplay (William Peter Blatty) and best sound (Robert Knidson and Chris Newman).

Warners' profits rose again in 1975 to over forty-one million dollars, and the studio was back in the Oscar business. *Barry Lyndon* won five Academy Awards – best cinematography (John Alcott), best art direction (Ken Adam and Roy Walker), best set decoration (Vernon Dixon), best costume design (Milena Canonero) and best music scoring and adaptation (Leonard Rosenman). Frank Pierson won the best original screenplay Oscar for his movie about two incompetent bank robbers *Dog Day Afternoon*.

Nineteen seventy-six was another banner Oscar year for Warners. And *All the President's Men* won them – for best supporting actor (Jason Robards), best screenplay adaptation (William Goldman), best art direction (George Jenkins), best set decoration (George Gaines) and best sound (Arthur Piantadosi, Les Fresholtz, Dick Alexander and Jim Webb). Profits rose to over forty-two million dollars.

Richard Dreyfuss won the only Academy Award for Warners in 1977, as best actor in *The Goodbye Girl*, and profits rose to over fifty-seven million dollars. Profits were up to over eighty-seven million dollars in 1978, but tragedy hit the studio when Jack Warner died that year. It was the end of an era.

Woodstock (1970) was a documentary about the legendary rock concert that took place over a period of three days on a farm near Bethel, New York, in 1969. Half a million people, as well as the cameras, were there. The audience was the star of this movie, although there were performances by scores of

Below: *A scene from* Woodstock *(1970), the documentary of the legendary rock concert held in New York in 1969.*

Above: *Robert Duvall, playing the title role in* THX 1138 *(1971), with his pursuers. This was the first film by George Lucas to be released.*

Right: *Joan Crawford tries sedation in* Trog *(1970).*
Previous spread: *Christopher Reeve, as The Man of Steel, in* Superman: The Movie *(1978).*

personalities and rock groups: Richie Havens, Joan Baez, The Who, Sha Na Na, Arlo Guthrie, Sly and the Family Stone and Jimi Hendrix. The editing job was the most sensational thing about the film, since 120 hours worth of rushes had to be cut down to 184 minutes running time.

Trog (1970) was a picture so bad that it was good. In the film, George Cornelius played the part of a man-ape – a huge-headed underground troglodyte – who is discovered by Joan Crawford, who tries to tame him. But villain Michael Gough works his evil on the creature, who, à la King Kong, abducts Chlöe Franks to his lair. The film was so ridiculous that even Joan Crawford couldn't save it.

Fledgling film-maker George Lucas got his start in 1971 with the theatrical release of *THX 1138*, based on a short work he had produced as a student at the University of Southern California. Concerning a future Sovereign State that controls the lives of its underground inhabitants, the film starred Robert Duvall as a worker whose daily drug dose is inadvertently diminished. Faced with stark reality, Duvall (THX 1138) becomes a fugitive on the run. Only after the State determines that it is over-budget in chasing him does it allow him to escape to the surface.

One of the most grotesque movies of all time was Warners' *The Devils* (1971), based on a stage play of the same name by John Whiting and on Aldous Huxley's novel, *The Devils of Loudon*, which, in turn, was based on an actual occurrence in France in 1633. Father Urbain Grandier, the handsome and worldly priest of the small town of Loudon in central France, was accused by the prioress of the local Ursaline convent of

bewitching her and several nuns. In the presence of their confessors, and later before huge crowds, the nuns threw themselves into convulsions, cursed God, lifted up their habits and coarsely invited sexual overtures from the shocked but fascinated onlookers.

At Grandier's trial, the prosecution produced a pact allegedly made between him and the Devil. Grandier was convicted as a witch and burned to death. Later it was discovered that Grandier had offended the all-powerful Cardinal Richelieu, and the nun's spiritual advisors had coached them in the proper 'possessed behavior' at the beginning, although they must have believed that they were possessed at the end.

Oliver Reed played the part of Grandier, and Vanessa Redgrave was Sister Jeanne, the nun who led the other sisters in unspeakable perversions, tortures, humiliations, degradations and sadism. It was a technically proficient mess –

Opposite: *Clint Eastwood (center) was San Francisco detective Harry Callahan in* Dirty Harry *(1971) – an investigative cop.*

Below: *Vanessa Redgrave played the prioress of a convent in France who accuses a priest of witchcraft in* The Devils *(1971).*

sacrilegious and in terrible taste. The critic Stanley Kauffman spoke for his colleagues: '[Ken] Russell's swirling multi-colored puddle . . . made me glad that both Huxley and Whiting are dead, so that they are spared this farrago of witless exhibitionism.'

Jane Fonda was merely magnificent – winning the Academy Award for best actress – in *Klute* (1971), the story of a prostitute who aids a private detective (Donald Sutherland) in solving a case about a missing person. The picture was truly an adult thriller, although the ending didn't quite ring true as Fonda is saved from the clutches of the villain by Sutherland just in the nick of time. Also in the cast were Charles Cioffi, Roy Scheider, Dorothy Tristan and Rita Gam.

Dirty Harry (1971) was the first film to feature the amoral, yet incorruptible Clint Eastwood as a detective on the San Francisco police force. This movie really broke the violence barrier in films, and had the public clamoring for more and more ultra-brutal 'dirty cop' pictures. In the film, Dirty Harry Callahan tracks down a thoroughly disgusting sniper. It was a grim, riveting movie, and featured Harry Guardino, Reni Santoni (as Harry's partner), Andy Robinson (as the sniper), John Larch, John Vernon and John Mitchum.

Warners made another important science fiction film in 1971, *A Clockwork Orange*, director Stanley Kubrick's third foray into the genre. Based on Anthony Burgess' novel, the film sends a highly pessimistic message about our culture, which both breeds and barbarically suppresses violence. The conditioning of an incorrigible gangster to abhor violence, with techniques that are equally inhumane, backfires. Malcolm McDowell delivered a chilling performance as the criminal savage, who, despite his utter lack of morality, deserves pity as the victim of a ruthless, immoral government and its self-centered manipulation of the people. The picture turned out to be a splendid political allegory that managed to concoct some of the most repellant scenes ever put on film, envisioning a future society ravished by juvenile gangs.

Charlton Heston went from starring in Biblical epics in his early career to appearing in science fiction films, such as *The Omega Man* (1971). In this film, directed by Boris Sagal, he portrayed the sole survivor of a plague that has transformed the rest of the world's population into violent, germ-ridden albino creatures. Heston's character, a scientist who acci-

Right: *Charlton Heston, as Robert Neville, a medical researcher and the last normal man on earth, confronts the leader of the diseased albino tribe (Anthony Zerbe) in* The Omega Man *(1971).*
Opposite top: *Malcolm McDowell as the young gang leader in* A Clockwork Orange *(1971). He was altogether chilling as the pathological hoodlum.*

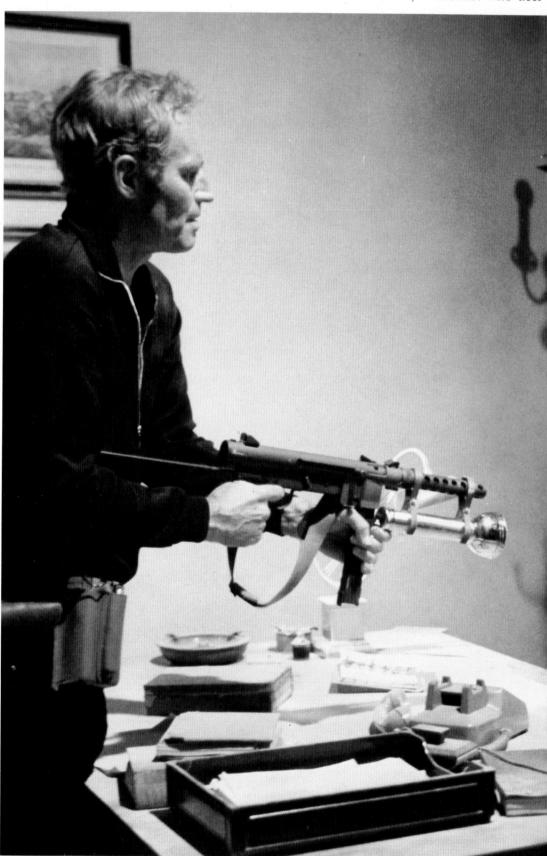

Opposite bottom: *A scene from* A Clockwork Orange *(1971) in which the gang molests an old man. The film was a shattering political allegory about a loathsome, violent anti-hero in a modern society where young punks run amok and peaceful citizens are prisoners in their own homes.*

dentally helped to create the disease, must wage an almost helpless one-man war against the creatures, and all the time he works on an antidote for the plague.

Summer of '42 (1971) was a sensitive trip down memory lane which ran against the current trend toward violence. It told of the growing pains of three teen-age boys who are spending a holiday with their families off the coast of New England. One of them, Hermie (Gary Grimes), falls in love with an older woman, a beautiful 22-year-old (Jennifer O'Neill), and grows from boyhood to manhood in an era when seeing a female breast or looking at a sex manual was almost as good as the real thing. The other two boys were played by Jerry Houser and Oliver Conant in this movie that brought back the early 1940s and its morality.

Robert Redford starred in *The Candidate* (1972) as an idealistic California lawyer who wins an upset victory in an election for the United States Senate. Of course this changes his life and, ultimately, his moral code. This was one of the first films in which Redford got to prove that he was more than just a pretty face. Also in the cast were Karen Carlson (as the wife he alienates during the campaign), Peter Boyle, Melvyn Douglas and Don Porter.

Another Robert Redford film of 1972 was *Jeremiah Johnson*. He played the title role, that of a mid-nineteenth century army veteran who moved to the mountains for some peace and quiet. But he wound up having to fight a constant battle with Indians and the elements. The most important thing about this movie, aside from the sweeping scenic panoramas and the fine acting by Redford, was the battle that director Sydney Pollack waged with the studio. Warners wanted it shot on the back lot and Pollack wanted it shot on location. Finally, Pollack was allowed to shoot in the Utah mountains only if he could bring the picture in under the amount that

Above: *Attacks by marauding Indians were only part of the difficulties that* Jeremiah Johnson *(1972) faced. Robert Redford also had to put up with subzero weather, blizzards and wolf packs.*

Left: *Burt Reynolds in* Deliverance *(1972). The film was based on the novel by James Dickey.*

Opposite: *Robert DeNiro (left) talks with his sister's boy friend, Harvey Keitel in* Mean Streets *(1973), a story of crime in Manhattan's Little Italy.*

would have been spent if it had been filmed in the Burbank studios. His gamble paid off, and the picture netted over $22 million.

Deliverance (1972), based on the novel by James Dickey, told of four suburban Atlanta friends who spend a weekend on a canoeing trip in the Appalachians. Along the way, they are attacked by mountain men, one of them is sodomized, and the four realize that only through committing murder can they get out alive. Some of the scenes were thrilling, with them battling rapids, climbing cliffs and lying in wait for their enemies. Starring as the four friends and giving fine performances were Burt Reynolds, Jon Voight, Ned Beatty and Ronny Cox.

Paul Newman starred in John Huston's *The Mackintosh Man* (1973) as a British intelligence agent who frames himself and gets sent to prison to do some undercover work. He is after a master spy who is also a member of Parliament (James Mason). After escaping from prison with another spy whom he has befriended, Newman, in a convoluted plot that would have pleased any spy thriller aficionado, unmasks the archfiend. Also in the cast were Dominique Sanda (also an agent), Harry Andrews, Nigel Patrick and Roland Culver.

Mean Streets (1973) was director Martin Scorsese's third movie, and he did a fine job, mostly because he was telling about a neighborhood that he knew intimately – New York's Little Italy. The film told the story of a second-generation Italian-American (Harvey Keitel) who suffers from religious guilt and family loyalty even as he is climbing the Mafia ladder. It turns out that he is not tough enough to succeed in his life of crime. Amy Robinson was his epileptic girl friend and Robert De Niro played the part of her brother – a man who makes the mistake of dealing with loan sharks. It was a powerful film – a most harrowing picture.

Then came the picture that everyone was looking forward to – *The Exorcist* (1973). Like *Rosemary's Baby*, William Friedkin's *Exorcist* was based on a best-selling novel by William Peter Blatty, and the book itself was allegedly based on a true story. It is doubtful that either the book or the movie bore any significant relationship to anything that actually had happened, but the fact that it was supposed to be somewhat true did give the film an extra advantage in the area of publicity.

The picture tells the story of a young girl, Regan, played by Linda Blair, who becomes possessed by a demon – the

Opposite: *Regan (played by Linda Blair) exhibits the evil transformations made by a demon in* The Exorcist *(1973)*.

Above: *Father Karras (Jason Miller) becomes the unwilling assistant in the rites of exorcism in* The Exorcist *(1973)*.

demon's voice is that of veteran actress Mercedes McCambridge and is the most consistently creepy element of the film. The demon causes the girl to do many strange things. She can turn her head completely around, she levitates, she causes the bed to rock back and forth, she curses, she vomits (although it looks like pea soup), she develops self-inflicted wounds. Regan's mother (Ellen Burstyn) finally gains the help of an exorcist – a priest played by Max Von Sydow, who struggles to free the girl from the Devil.

The film's release was preceded by an extraordinary amount of publicity, and it quickly became the biggest box office grosser of any horror film in history. People lined up around the block in all sorts of weather to buy tickets. *The Exorcist* was the most talked-about picture of its day, a movie that people just *had* to see, if they could stand it. For years, studio publicists had issued claims that this or that horror film was so terrifying that members of the audience fainted or fled the theater screaming. The same sort of claims were made about *The Exorcist*, and at least some of them appeared to be true. The difference was that instead of being frightened out of the theater, people had to leave because they were feeling disgusted or sick.

The criticism that the film had 'gone too far' did not keep people away from the theaters one bit. If the public wanted horrific shock, the movie makers were ever ready to give it to them. Actually, *The Exorcist* had a lot more going for it than a couple of shocking scenes. It was a well-acted, tightly-directed movie that still holds up, and can now be considered a genuine horror classic.

Badlands (1974) was a film perfect for the 1970s' feeling of disenchantment, although the picture was set in the 1950s. It was based on the real life career of Charles Starkweather and his 14-year-old girl friend who, in 1958, killed ten people in a crime spree in the Plains States. He was captured and died in the electric chair, and his girl friend was sentenced to life in prison. In the movie, Martin Sheen played Kit Carruthers, a 25-year-old garbage collector who thought he looked like James Dean (and he did), and his girl friend, Holly Sargis, a 15-year-old baton twirler from South Dakota, was played by Sissy Spacek. They start their killings close at home, with Holly's father (Warren Oates), a man who disapproves of their attachment to each other, being the first victim. Then they go on to kill five more people by shooting them at point-blank range. The actors all gave totally convincing performances in this grim, bloody tale of violence and horror.

Mame premiered on Broadway in 1966. The book was by Jerome Lawrence and Robert E Lee and, of course, was based on Patrick Dennis's novel, play and film, *Auntie Mame*. The words and music were by Jerry Herman. Directed by Gene Saks, with dances by Onna White, it starred Angela Lansbury, Frankie Michaels, Beatrice Arthur, Jane Connell and Willard Waterman, and ran for 1508 performances.

Warners' film version of *Mame* (1974) was another dilution of a smash Broadway show. Lucille Ball was Mame, Beatrice Arthur re-created her Broadway role as Mame's actress friend, Vera Charles, and Robert Preston was Mame's Southern beau, Beauregard Jackson Pickett Burnside. Un-

Above: *Martin Sheen (looking remarkably like James Dean) and Sissy Spacek, as the two cold-blooded killers, Kit Carruthers and Holly Sargis, in* Badlands *(1974).*
Left: *Lucille Ball, as the irrepressible* Mame *(1974) performs at one of her parties.*

Opposite right: *Gene Wilder (left), as Jim, the Waco Kid, has a difference of opinion with Cleavon Little, as his friend, the sheriff in* Blazing Saddles *(1974).*
Opposite far right: *Lucille Ball as* Mame *(1974) in her trumpet routine, 'It's Today'.*

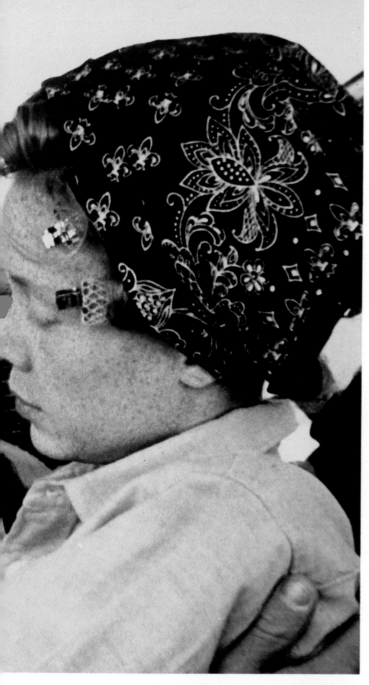

fortunately, Lucille Ball didn't measure up to the sophisticated grandness and exaggerated madness of the larger-than-life character, at least not in the manner of such previous Auntie Mames as Angela Lansbury and Rosalind Russell.

Mel Brooks was at his best in *Blazing Saddles* (1974), a mèlange of sight gags, one-liners, blackout sketches, parody, satire and farce. He co-wrote the film, directed it and appeared in it (as a territorial governor and a Yiddish-speaking Indian chief). The story line, such as it was, involved Bart, a

black sheriff (Cleavon Little), and his white sidekick Jim, the Waco Kid (Gene Wilder), who save the town of Ridge Rock from land speculators, meanwhile having all the hackneyed adventures ever seen in a Western movie. Harvey Korman played Hedley Lamarr, a crooked business tycoon, and Alex Karras was the beagle-brained desperado, Mongo, who is able to knock horses unconscious with a single blow. Madeline Kahn was the lisping dance hall singer, Lily von Shtupp, who sang 'I'm Tired' in a way to give Marlene Dietrich in *Destry Rides Again* a run for her money. The movie had many wonderfully zany scenes. An all-black railroad construction gang lays track while giving a rendition of Cole Porter's 'I Get a Kick out of You.' Lily responds to the present of a flower by saying 'Oh, a wed wose! How womantic!' A bigoted preacher

Left: *Steve McQueen, as the fire-fighter, in a moment of decision in fighting the fire in* The Towering Inferno *(1974).*

Above: *Madeline Kahn, as the entertainer, Lily von Shtupp, sings 'I'm Tired' in* Blazing Saddles *(1974).*

(Liam Dunn) decries the fate of the town by saying '. . . our people scattered, our cattle raped . . .' Most of the film worked, and Brooks fans were ecstatic, even though the last scene was a hodge-podge of time travel that indicated that the man didn't know how to end the movie.

The posters trumpeted, 'One tiny spark becomes a night of blazing suspense. The world's tallest building is on fire. You are there on the 135th floor . . . no way down . . . no way out.' Warners and Twentieth Century-Fox paired in a one-shot marriage of convenience to finance *The Towering Inferno* (1974), a three-hour suspense film seemingly made for arsonists, firemen, movie-technology buffs, building inspectors and worry warts. Actually, the picture was the best of all the disaster films so popular in the 1970s, although it was a typical one. First we are introduced to the motley cast and then they are abandoned to their fate – this time being trapped in a burning San Francisco skyscraper. The fire comes as a result of faulty wiring installed when the builder tried to cut costs. Of course the good guys are saved and the bad guys perish. The picture had an all-star cast. Paul Newman was the architect, Faye Dunaway was a magazine editor, Richard Chamberlain was responsible for the wiring, Susan Blakely was his wife, Robert Vaughn was a United States Senator, Robert Wagner was the building's public relations man, Fred Astaire was an aging con man, Jennifer Jones was a widowed art dealer, Steve McQueen was the head fireman, William Holden was the building's developer and O J Simpson was a security guard. Audiences loved it more than most disaster films because they felt closer to it. There is more likelihood of being trapped in a burning building than there is being stuck in a sinking ship, an aircraft in distress or an earthquake.

Ellen Burstyn stole *Alice Doesn't Live Here Anymore* (1975) with her vibrant, unsentimental performance as a poor 35-year-old widow who, after her husband (Billy Green Bush) dies, heads west with her 12-year-old son (Alfred Lutter). She hopes to make it big as a singer, but ends up as waitress in a diner in Tucson, Arizona. Martin Scorsese direction did the most to make audiences believe i Burstyn's anger and frustration. Also in the cast were Harve Keitel, Kris Kristofferson, Diane Ladd, Jodie Foster and Vi Tayback, who went on to star with Linda Lavin in the tele vision sit-com version of the movie – 'Alice.'

The posters explained it – 'The robbery should have take ten minutes. Four hours later, the bank was like a circu sideshow. Eight hours later, it was the hottest thing on liv TV. Twelve hours later, it was history. And it's all true.' *Do Day Afternoon* (1975) was a powerful film that had aud ences sitting on the edges of their seats. Sonny (Al Pacino had nothing going for him – he had debts, his wife wa unhappy, his male lover wanted money for a sex-chang operation. So he teams up with a slightly deranged friend, Sa (John Cazale), and tries to rob a bank in Brooklyn. When th heist misfires, the two hole up in the bank with their hostage – the bank employees. The incident on which the film wa based was a similar attempt to rob a branch of the Chas Manhattan Bank on 22 August 1972. The movie started out a a farce, but gradually became a serious drama, concentratin; on the relationships that developed between the robbers an the hostages, and even managed to make the two would-b criminals into sympathetic losers. Pacino was mesmerizin;

Above: *Al Pacino proves to the police that he is holding some bank employees including Penny Allen hostage in* Dog Day Afternoon *(1975).*
Opposite: *Kris Kristofferson and Ellen Burstyn in a happy moment in the diner in* Alice Doesn't Live Here Anymore *(1975).*

Right: *A discouraged pair – John Cazale (left) and Al Pacino as the inept bank robbers in* Dog Day Afternoon *(1975).*

and Cazale was great. Also giving fine performances were Chris Sarandon as Leon, the drag-queen lover, and Susan Peretz as Angie, Sonny's wife. James Broderick as Sheldon, the federal agent, and Charles Durning as Moretti, the New York detective, were also fine.

Stanley Kubrick was the writer-producer-director of the beautifully produced *Barry Lyndon* (1975), based on the Thackeray novel. The film told of the picaresque adventures of Redmond Barry, a young Irishman (Ryan O'Neal), who strives to climb the social ladder in eighteenth-century England. He flees from a duel and joins the British Army, deserts, and marries Lady Lyndon, a wealthy widow (Marisa Berenson). He mistreats her and her son by her first marriage, but controls the estate anyway. His greed, egotism and ambition cause his downfall, and he ends up destitute and minus a leg.

Robert Redford and Dustin Hoffman were perfect as Bob Woodward and Carl Bernstein of the *Washington Post* in *All The President's Men* (1976). These were the two reporters whose fearless and painstaking investigation exposed the Watergate scandal. The film told of the backbreaking job of reporting that these two men did, and the picture became a compelling thriller. The two superstars were completely believable, as were Jason Robards as *Post* editor Ben Bradlee,

Jack Warden as Harry Rosenfield, and Martin Balsam, Jane Alexander and Hal Holbrook.

Art Carney and Lily Tomlin were nearly perfect in *The Late Show* (1977) – a tribute to Raymond Chandler's thrillers. Carney played a paunchy old former private detective who had to retire because of a game leg, a weak heart, deafness and bad eyesight. Then one day his ex-partner (Howard Duff) enters with a bullet in his stomach and dies on the spot. Tomlin played the part of a flaky girl who becomes sentimentally attached to Carney and assists him in solving the crime.

The Goodbye Girl (1977) had an original screenplay by Neil Simon and starred his then-wife Marsha Mason, as Paula McFadden, and Richard Dreyfuss as aspiring actor Elliot Garfield (Dreyfuss won the best actor Academy Award for the film). Mason's ex-lover has sublet their apartment to Dreyfuss without telling her about it, and Dreyfuss moves in. The story went on to tell of the growing relationship between the two, beginning when Dreyfuss shows up unexpectedly in the middle of the night to move in. Quinn Cummings was Mason's precocious daughter and Paul Benedict was an off-Broadway director who has Dreyfuss play Richard III as if he were gay. This was a Warner Bros.-MGM co-production.

Superman: The Movie (1978) had taken two years to make,

Above: *Robert Redford (left) as Bob Woodward, and Dustin Hoffman as Carl Bernstein – the two* Washington Post *reporters who broke the Watergate scandal – in* All The President's Men *(1976).*

Opposite: *Ryan O'Neal and Marisa Berenson relaxing in a punt in Stanley Kubrick's lavish production of* Barry Lyndon *(1975).*

Right: *Richard Dreyfuss and Marsha Mason are unperturbed by a rain shower on their rooftop dinner table in* The Goodbye Girl *(1977).*

Above: *Christopher Reeve, as Clark Kent (a.k.a. Superman), calls on Margot Kidder, as Lois Lane in* Superman: The Movie *(1978).*
Right: *Christopher Reeve as the Man of Steel, flies over Gotham City in* Superman: The Movie *(1978).*

with location work in New York City; Gallup, New Mexico; Alberta, Canada; and at Shepperton and Pinewood Studios in England. And the final budget had hit $40 million. Marlon Brando was signed to play Superman's father, Jor-El, for $3 million alone, which, because of his 13-day shooting schedule, came out to about $480 per minute. The producers wanted Robert Redford to play Superman, but he wanted more money and a finished script. Paul Newman also declined, and the studio offered him a counter-role as the villain, Lex Luthor, which he also turned down. Gene Hackman was picked for Luthor and was paid $2 million, but he worked harder than Brando had. After Newman, the following declined the role as Superman: Clint Eastwood, Steve McQueen, Charles Bronson, Ryan O'Neal, Sylvester Stallone, Burt Reynolds, Nick Nolte, Jan Michael Vincent, David Soul, Kris Kristofferson and Robert Wagner. The lucky last choice was Christopher Reeve, who was ideal. He was handsome, had done stage work, was not typecast and was willing to work out on a fitness program, lifting weights two hours a day, doing roadwork in the morning and spending one and a half hours on the trampoline. Lois Lane was another tough role to cast. It was turned down by Jill Clayburgh, Jessica Lange, Liza Minnelli, Shirley MacLaine, Natalie Wood and Carrie Fisher, either because of lack of interest or unavailability. Finally the role went to Margot Kidder, an accomplished actress.

Above: *Marlon Brando, as Jor-El, and Susannah York, as Lara, seen on Krypton prepare to send their son into space in* Superman: The Movie *(1978).*

Opposite: *Malcolm McDowell played H G Wells, here seen in his time machine in* Time After Time *(1979), on his way to find Jack the Ripper.*

The film turned out to be a delightful romp, a real take-off, a funny movie. The plot line of the main part of the movie (Superman's departure from the planet Krypton and his adoption by an Iowa farm family were the first two short sections) concerned Lex Luthor's plot to buy Arizona land and then cause an earthquake to destroy California, thus giving him miles of oceanfront property. The picture also featured Ned Beatty and Valerie Perrine as Luthor's useless assistants. Glenn Ford and Phyllis Thaxter were Superman's Iowa parents, Jackie Cooper was Perry White, the editor of the *Daily Planet*, Susannah York was Superman's real mother, Lara. *Superman: The Movie* was a triumph and was loved by young and old alike. The special effects won a deserved special Oscar.

Malcolm McDowell starred as H G Wells in *Time After Time* (1979). The movie borrowed the machine, but not the plot, from a novelette by Wells – *The Time Machine*. The plot of the picture was fun, but rather complicated. Wells has invented a time machine that will take him either into the past or the future. He demonstrates the machine to a group of his friends, not knowing that one of them (David Warner) is actually Jack the Ripper. When the police arrive to arrest the criminal, he steals the machine and travels to the future, sending the machine back after he alights in the San Francisco of 1979. Wells now can follow him, and does. Wells captures Jack the Ripper, sends him to the outer spheres of the galaxy, and returns to Victorian England with the San Francisco girl he has fallen in love with. The engaging premise was filled with loopholes in the story and some half-hearted attempts at social comment. Mary Steenburgen was especially effective as Wells' modern girl friend.

In a sense, the end of the seventies was an end of an era for Warners. It was the end of the studio's being in the vanguard of movie making: The bottom line had taken over.

THE
EIGHTIES

TIME WAS WHEN ACTORS at such studios as Warner Bros. were placed under contract at specified salaries for 40 weeks per year. Hollywood in the 1980s consists of actors who are also their own producers and who insist on million-dollar guarantees, a sizable share of the picture's profit and artistic control of the product – all without risking any of their own capital. The inmates have taken over the asylum, and no longer does a film company have control. This is the era when Sylvester Stallone can ask for, and get, $12 million up front, Robert Redford $6 million, Goldie Hawn and Meryl Streep $3 million and even young Michael J Fox can get $1.5 million.

The big studios, and this includes Warners, are looking for money – not only from their films, but also from video cassettes, cable television, syndication and any other place they can get it. Major studios are able to weather bad years at the theatrical box office because of the money earned by their television production and syndication divisions.

Warners made some good and entertaining films in the first half of the decade but did not fare too well in the Academy Awards department. The film that took the most Oscars was not a financial success. It was *The Right Stuff* (1983), and the awards were for original score, editing, sound and sound effects editing – not exactly what it was like

in the good old days. The studio also went into co-production, most often with Ladd and Orion.

The most profitable films for many of the studios were sequels of previous hits. Warner Bros. made *Superman II* and *III*. The audience appetite seemed insatiable and only the defection of Christopher Reeve stopped *Superman IV*.

Tom Horn (1980) was one of the last two films that Steve McQueen made before his death from cancer in 1980. McQueen reportedly became interested in a film about Tom Horn because of his interest in Western history. Horn was one of the last of the bounty hunters in the West. At the turn of the century, when most other gunmen were dead or retired, Horn was still killing rustlers. But he, too, outlived his time and met a tragic end.

The movie, directed by William Wiard, told about Tom Horn's last days in a raw Wyoming town. The new breed of men who run such towns was made up of businessmen who set up Chambers of Commerce, subdivide rangeland and sell it. They hired Horn to wipe out a menacing gang of rustlers because of his reputation as a fearless and ruthless gunman who kills for pay. Horn does his job with his usual efficiency, but his killing skills and his cantankerous independence make the businessmen afraid that they won't be able to make

him do what they want in the future. He is regarded as a danger to them, so they frame him for the murder of a teenage boy. They know just how to set the machinery of the law in motion, with the cooperation of the sheriff, and they succeed in jailing Horn. The film takes its time in showing how hopeless is Horn's fight to prove his innocence. It also moves at a deliberate pace in showing his execution, his cool courage and the mixed emotions of his executioners.

McQueen gave a moving and believable performance as the gunman who becomes resigned to his fate. His weather-beaten features and his quiet underplaying of the role were very effective in an emotional story. Director Wiard did a fine job of fashioning a good, solid Western with a tragic message.

In *The Shining* (1980), based on the Stephen King novel, Jack Nicholson played the part of an alcoholic writer, Jack Torrance, struggling for sobriety. He and his wife, Wendy (Shelley Duvall), and their young son, Danny (Danny Lloyd), are the winter caretakers in an isolated Colorado mountain spa, the Overlook Hotel, where Jack hopes to fight the demon rum and finish his book. When they arrive at the hotel, Danny meets the cook (Scatman Crothers), who reveals to him that they both have the gift of telepathy. Crothers goes off to his winter holiday in Florida. As the weeks go on, and the hotel gets snowed in, Jack goes off the deep end. The ghosts of evil former guests begin to appear in his mind and eventually he finds himself in the Gold Room of the hotel at the fourth of July Ball in 1921. He is given some drinks by the ghostly bartender, Lloyd, and runs into Delbert Grady, a waiter who had, long ago, chopped up his two daughters and his wife in the hotel. Meanwhile, Danny has had some encounters with the ghosts of the children. Grady convinces Jack that he should discipline his family by chopping them up, too, and Jack sets out to do this. Danny sends telepathic messages to the cook, and Jack chops the door to their suite down with an axe, screaming 'Here's Johnny!'

Wendy and Danny escape and the cook arrives, having flown to Denver and stolen a snow vehicle. But he is killed by Jack, and the mother and son escape in the snow vehicle.

Probably the most horrifying scene in the film was not the episode where Jack meets a nude woman in her room, only to have her turned into a drowned hag lying in the bathtub, nor was it Danny's encounters with the dead sisters or the blood that gushed out of the elevator. It was when Jack's wife, not knowing that he is mad, looks at the stack of papers that Jack has typed. She thinks that he has been working on his manuscript, but it turns out that every page has nothing on it but 'All work and no play makes Jack a dull boy' typed over and over – single-spaced, double-spaced, in the shape of an inverted Christmas tree and every other style that the mind can imagine.

Left: *Jack Nicholson chases his son through the topiary maze during a snowstorm in* The Shining *(1980).*

Above: *Nicholson, as the insane Jack Torrance, manages to chop a hole in the bathroom door in* The Shining *(1980).*

179

The Shining was supposed to be a major film event. Stephen King movies are always popular, and it was directed by Stanley Kubrick, acknowledged as one of the world's great directors, who had been working on the film for three years. Jack Nicholson was a fine actor as well as a hot film property. When *The Shining* was released, it turned out not to be quite the bone-chilling triumph that horror-movie buffs had been hoping for. No question that it contained many impressive moments and a couple of scenes that will linger in nightmares for years to come. Yet in the end there was a confusion about the film; Too many promising beginnings became dead ends. Supernatural horror does not have to be entirely logical, but a script should have a certain internal consistency and coherence. To a degree, *The Shining* lacked this. Nicholson gave a bravura performance as the writer rapidly being transformed into an axe-wielding madman. But perhaps Nicholson's performance was a bit too bravura. Shelley Duvall, his pathetic and irritating wife, was really better. Whatever one thinks of *The Shining*, however, it is no formula horror film, turned out to make the quick dollar. It will be closely studied by those interested in films, horror and otherwise, for many years to come.

Private Benjamin (1980) was a triumph for Goldie Hawn. She was terrific in this tailor-made vehicle (which she produced) that was later made into a television series. Her charming pout and her big blue eyes carried the action along from one laugh to another. The movie told the story of a bubble-headed Jewish-American Princess, widowed on her wedding night, who joins the Army. After a disastrous initiation, she finds direction and self-esteem for the first time in her life. It was an entertaining comedy with more substance than it was given credit for. Also in the cast were Eileen Brennan (who went on to the television series) as her captain, Armand Assante, Robert Webber as the post commander, Sam Wanamaker, Barbara Barrie, Mary Kay Place, Harry Dean Stanton and Albert Brooks.

Outland (1981) was a big-budget science-fiction picture with a high-technology look, written and directed by Peter Hyams. Sean Connery, the screen's former James Bond, starred as a Federal Space Marshal, sent out to Io, one of Jupiter's moons, to clean up the act of a boisterous mining colony. The management, led by Peter Boyle, has been involved in the sale of a dangerous amphetamine which increases worker productivity, but also causes lethal bursts of violence.

After the set-up, *Outland* has the same plot as the Western, *High Noon*; Connery's pleas for help from the inhabitants are ignored, and he must face Boyle's team of henchmen single-handedly. Audiences were somewhat disappointed at the end when, after a suspenseful chase and showdown, all Connery does to show his vengeance is punch Boyle in the

Below: *Sean Connery (right), as the Federal Space Marshal, overwhelms one of the miners in* Outland *(1981).*

Opposite: *Goldie Hawn, as the perky Jewish-American Princess who joins the Army in* Private Benjamin *(1980).*

nose. This does not seem to be enough gut feeling for him to have put so much at stake in the first place, considering his wife and child have walked out on him. Otherwise, the film was exciting, and the sets, designed by Philip Harrison, were 'high-tech' design brought to its ultimate use. The colony is a twisting, dark, grimy mass of steel girders and plastics. Noteworthy as the marshal's only friend was a middle-aged doctor, played with humor by Frances Sternhagen, *Outland's* comic relief.

Personal Best (1982) was an interesting film in that it explored a lesbian relationship in a sensitive way, but it did cop out when one of the women finds that she prefers men. Mariel Hemingway and Patrice Donnelly are two athletes in training for the 1980 Olympics who fall in love. The direction by Robert Towne was haphazard. He was excellent when it came to communicating human feelings. Particularly effective was the delineation of the women's relationships with their manipulative coach, Scott Glenn. But when the athletic training scenes came along, the director seemed to have a foot fetish.

Critics were split about *Firefox* (1982), some of them calling it Clint Eastwood's worst, while others characterized

Above: *Mary Beth Hurt hands her baby to her mother-in-law, Glenn Close, while Robin Williams, as proud father Garp, watches, in* The World According to Garp *(1982).*

it as being full of excitement. It was farfetched, but Eastwood was Eastwood, and that was enough for his fans. He played a burned-out American pilot who goes behind Russian lines to steal the Soviets' latest aeronautical marvel – a supersonic fighter plane that cannot be detected by radar. One reviewer gave Freddie Jones, who played the second lead, the 'Charles Laughton Award for Eccentric Performances.'

Death Trap (1982) starred Michael Caine, Christopher Reeve, Dyan Cannon, Irene Worth and Henry Jones, and was adapted from the long-running play with flair, excitement and top-notch performances. Caine played Sidney Bruhl, a has-been playwright who has been suffering through a series of flops. He receives a script through the mail from a young admirer (Reeve) and announces to his wife (Cannon) that he is going to kill the young man and pass the play off as his own. And that was just the beginning. The film took so many twists and turns that the audience was completely fooled until the final reel.

Warners came out with a dazzling adaptation of John Irving's eccentric novel, *The World According to Garp* (1982), starring Robin Williams, Mary Beth Hurt, Glenn Close, John Lithgow, Hume Cronyn, Jessica Tandy, Swoosie Kurtz and Amanda Plummer. It was the story of a young man's journey through life – an adventure shaped in a large part by

183

Above: *John Lithgow thinks he sees a gremlin on the wing of the commercial jet he is traveling on in* The Twilight Zone: The Movie *(1983).*

Opposite: *Mel Gibson looks for trouble as Mad Max in* The Road Warrior *(1982).*

Left: *Vic Morrow is in trouble with the SS in* The Twilight Zone: The Movie *(1983).*

his unorthodox and unmarried mother. Williams and Close were perfect as this odd couple, in an absorbing, sure-footed odyssey through the vignettes of social observation, absurdist humor, satire and melodrama. Lithgow was hilarious but always believable as Roberta, the former football player who has undergone a sex change, and Mary Beth Hurt was excellent as Garp's wife.

The Road Warrior (1982) began its life as *Mad Max 2*, but the title was soon changed. It told the story of a loner's adventures in a barren and dangerous world of the future in this science fiction neo-Western. Mel Gibson starred in the title role as a sort of postapocalyptic Shane, reluctantly rescuing a band of settlers menaced in their oil refinery-cum-homestead by marauding bikers. It was a lively and stylish movie with a lot of fine chase and car-crash footage. Also in the cast were Bruce Spence, Vernon Wells, Emile Minty, Mike Preston, Virginia Hey and Kjell Nilsson.

The Twilight Zone: The Movie (1983) had something for everybody, although most critics thought that it was a disappointing salute to Rod Serling's television cult classic series. Actually the film consisted of four short stories. The first was a diatribe about bigotry (Vic Morrow and two children were killed by a helicopter crash on the set during filming, which, of course, diluted the audience's reaction to the piece). The second part starred Scatman Crothers as a magician who turns the miserable tenants of an old folks home into children. They become idyllically happy, which led one critic to suggest that Steven Spielberg, the director, needed a vacation from uplifting movies about children.

Things got under way in the third episode about a teacher who finds herself in the home of a child who can work magic and has his family terrified because of it. The monstrous child eventually sends his sister to live in the world of Saturday-morning television cartoons, which makes his family even more obsequious. The best of the bunch was the fourth story, in which John Lithgow played the part of a passenger on an airliner who spots a gremlin on the wing destroying the plane in midflight. Lithgow was wonderful as the neurotic who disrupts the peace and quiet aboard the craft and becomes smug after he is proved to be sane after all.

Opposite: *The triumphant ticker-tape parade for the astronauts in* The Right Stuff *(1983).*

Above: *A serious moment in the training of the United States' first astronauts in* The Right Stuff *(1983).*

Somehow *The Right Stuff* (1983), based on Tom Woolf's best-selling non-fiction book, never got off the ground. The critics were impressed, but the public stayed away. It told the story of the development of the race for space and delved deeply into the lives of the Mercury astronauts while they were in training – actually turning them into human beings instead of media heroes.

Blue Skies Again (1983) was a sort of upbeat *Brian's Song* with a touch of *Breaking Away*. The swinging owner of a major league baseball team is told that a dynamic new second baseman is reporting to spring training and will become the answer to the team's batting and fielding problems. Instead, a young woman (Robyn Varto) shows up. She has a talent, but the sexist owner (Harry Hamlin) doesn't want to give her a tryout. The girl's agent prevails, but during the tryout the members of the team are so cruel that she flunks. After much soul-searching, the manager of the team, knowing that she is good enough to play, plots to sneak her into an exhibition game as a pinch hitter. She faces a tough unsmiling pitcher and finally gets an extra-base hit (in slow motion, of course). The warmth of the characterizations of most of the cast was wonderful, and the audiences really wanted that kid to be a success. And the tiny encouraging smile on the pitcher's face as he looks at her leading off second base was worth the price of admission.

Goldie Hawn starred as Sunny Davis in *Protocol* (1984). She was a Washington DC cocktail waitress who becomes a national celebrity when she saves the life of an Arabian potentate who is visiting the capital to discuss the possibility of letting the Air Force build a strategic base in his emirate. Sunny is given a job in the Protocol Bureau and assigned to show the king 'a good time.' Of course she does not know that the bureau is merely using her to cement good relations, and she doesn't find out until she finds herself in the Mid-East being groomed to become the latest wife of the king. An insurrection begins, and Sunny gets back to the United States and is summoned to appear before a Congressional Committee. Her speech about how she had been duped by her own government and her disgust with the underhanded chicanery she has discovered was one of the most moving parts of the film. She ends up being elected to Congress after

Left: *Goldie Hawn, as Sunny Davis, gives an interview in* Protocol *(1984). To the left is Gail Strickland as the scheming protocol chief.*
Opposite top: *Celie (Whoopi Goldberg) is separated from her sister Nettie (Akosua Busia) by her violent common-law husband (Danny Glover) in* The Color Purple *(1985).*

Opposite bottom: *Kate Nelligan, as* Eleni *(1985), helps the children to escape.*
Below: *Al Pacino, as patriot Tom Dobb, confronts the Redcoats in* Revolution *(1985).*

the 'Sunnygate Affair.' The script by Buck Henry was excellent, and one critic called it 'An absolutely marvelous movie. Pure pleasure from beginning to end.' while another raved about the 'delightful blend of *Born Yesterday* and *Mr Smith Goes to Washington.*' Hawn was splendid, and her excellent supporting cast included Richard Romanus as the king, Gail Strickland as the scheming protocol chief and Chris Sarandon as a protocol official who sees the light, quits his job and marries Sunny.

Sometimes a noble experiment in film making just doesn't work out. That was the case with *Revolution* (1985), a film about the American War for Independence. Al Pacino, terribly miscast with his twentieth-century New York accent, played Tom Dobb, a widowed farmer-trapper who leaves the Adirondacks to go to New York City and is caught up in the Revolution when his 14-year-old son (Sid Owen) is tortured by a sadistic British sergeant (Donald Sutherland). Tom joins the Army to be with his son, who has already enlisted as a drummer boy. Together they fight the Battles of Brooklyn Heights and Manhattan, put in an appearance at Valley Forge and are at hand for the surrender of Yorktown. The film, although beautifully photographed and with a cast of thousands, was a mess. Apart from the fact that the citizens in New York at the beginning of the film looked like they had just escaped from the *A Tale of Two Cities*' version of the Reign of Terror, it's difficult to understand why no notice was ever taken of the motivation behind the Revolution itself. For example, the Stamp Act and the Boston Tea Party are never

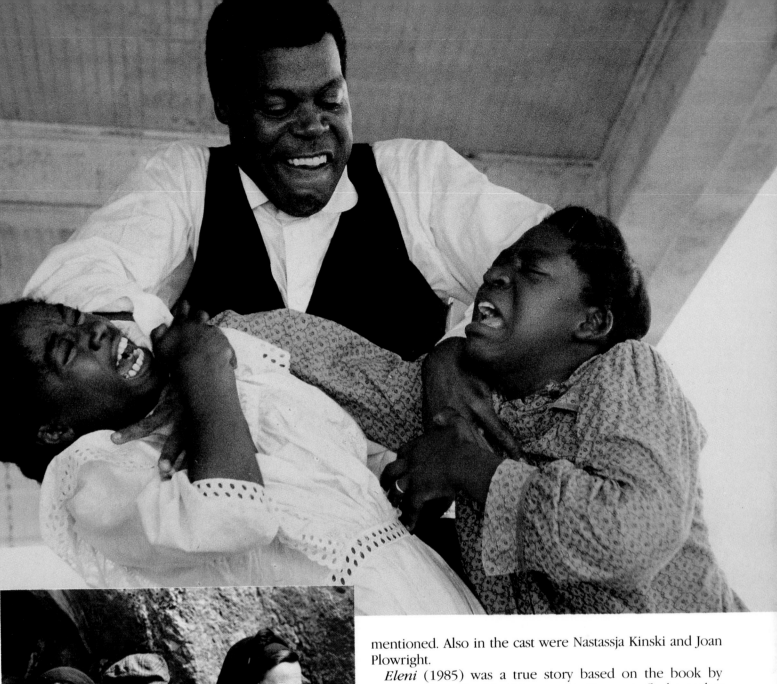

mentioned. Also in the cast were Nastassja Kinski and Joan Plowright.

Eleni (1985) was a true story based on the book by Nicholas Gage. It told of his return to Greece to find out what he can about his mother, Eleni, who had been able to get him away from the occupying troops and out of the country, but who was herself imprisoned and killed. He also is out to find the man who killed her. Kate Nelligan was magnificent in the title role, her scenes being told in flashback. John Malkovich was fine as Gage, *The New York Times* reporter. It was a riveting and shattering film.

Based on Alice Walker's novel, *The Color Purple* (1985) was either loved or hated. The barely literate Celie (Whoopi Goldberg), raped by her father at an early age, is abused by her cruel common-law husband (Danny Glover), whom she calls Mr, and is humanized by a bisexual blues singer named Shug Avery (Margaret Avery). There was hidden strength in Goldberg's riveting presence. Although the realism and grit of Walker's novel were missing, the film became an upbeat, affirmative fable in which optimism, patience and family loyalty emerge as cardinal virtues. Director Steven Speilberg didn't exactly hit the bullseye, but he wasn't far off.

And that is the story of Warner Bros. up to the middle of the 1980s. They have had their ups and downs – more ups than downs – and they have survived. At least they are still in the business of making movies, unlike some of their former rivals, and they have given us some classic films and hours of entertainment. May the studio rise again to its former heights.

Acknowledgments

All pictures from the Bison Books Collection except
The Museum of Modern Art: 10, 12, 14, 15, 18, 19, 20, 21 (top), 22, 24 (top), 27, 28 (left), 28-29, 29 (bottom), 31, 32-33, 35, 36, 38, 39, 47, 48, 49, 50 (top), 64 (bottom), 66-67, 69 (top), 80, 81, 83 (top), 98 (bottom), 100, 101, 104 (bottom), 118, 119, 122-123, 127 (bottom), 128-129, 130, 139, 144 (top), 146-147, 151 (bottom), 176, 189 (bottom)
National Film Archive, London: 2 (top and bottom left), 8-9, 11, 13, 25, 46, 51, 107, 121 (bottom), 155
Phototeque: 6, 16-17, 21 (bottom), 23, 24 (bottom), 26, 37 (top), 40, 57 (top), 58 (left), 69 (bottom), 90, 91, 126 (bottom), 132 (top), 157

The author and publisher would like to thank the following people who have helped in the preparation of this book: Alan Gooch, who designed it; Elizabeth Montgomery who edited it; Mary R Raho and Donna Cornell, who did the picture research; and Gisela Knight who prepared the index.